Jennifer
Keep The
Watking The
Walk

My Search for Christopher
on the Other Side

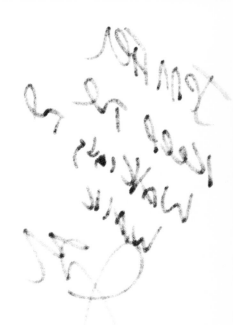

Published by Lisa Hagan Books 2018

www.lisahaganbooks.com

Powered by

SHADOW
TEAMS

Copyright © Joe McQuillen 2018

ISBN: 9781945962424

Cover design and interior layout by Simon Hartshorne

My Search for Christopher
on the
Other Side

Joe McQuillen

"Joe is proof that it's never too late to open up your intuition and experience miraculous messages from beyond. Do yourself a favor and follow his lead."
–Jenniffer Weigel, Author/Journalist

"The other side is real and there is no better feeling than going through life with this certainty. This book connects with the reader in a very accurate and truthful manner. I absolutely recommend Joe's book."
–Andrew Anderson, Psychic Medium

"A love so strong and deep between a father and son, you feel as though you are eavesdropping on them."
–Amy Leigh Mercree, medical intuitive and bestselling author of ten books including *A Little Bit of Mindfulness, Essential Oils Handbook, Apple Cider Vinegar Handbook, and A Little Bit of Meditation*

"A touching story of a family's great love, a tragic death within it, and the reshaping of enormous grief into spiritual reconnection from both sides of heaven."
–Nancine Meyer, a.k.a. Main Street Angel Certified Spiritual Teacher, Sixth Sensory Consultant, author of The Lighter Side of Prayer

"I am honored to have channeled Christopher for his father, Joe. The everlasting bond between father and son is beautiful to witness. The boundless love between Joe and Chris has been a blessing to experience."
– Sheri Jewel, psychic medium, energy healer, and angel card reader

"McQuillen bares his soul so that we may all heal from the loss of a loved one."
– Elaine Clayton, Intuitive and author of Making Marks, A Little Bit of Angels and A Little Bit of Fairies

CONTENTS

"Goodbyes are only for those who love with their eyes.
Because for those who love with heart and soul
there is no such thing as separation."

—Rumi

INTRODUCTION

On Jan 3, 2016, I sat surrounded by the evidence of Christmas. The tree was still up, there were, holiday cards in a basket on the end table and my son Christopher's new golf bag sat in the corner of the living room. It was a fine Christmas. One of the best. For some reason we (my wife Sally and I) kept piling on gifts. I even went back out to the mall early Christmas Eve to grab one more cologne gift set for Chris, a bottle of perfume for Caroline and shaving set for Will. Why not it was already over the top. Everybody was happy, and we knew this Christmas with us all together would be remembered. And it will be.

Along with a group of high school friends Chris spent the night at one of their parents' lake houses in Wisconsin an hour and a half away. A last hurrah before Christmas break ended and school started back up. Just after noon I received a call from one of Christopher's friend Scottie, whose parents owned the house telling me that Chris was missing. When the group woke up in the morning Chris and three of his friends were nowhere to be found. I had Scottie text me the address (I'm looking at the text now on my phone as I write this) and started driving north. About forty minutes into my drive I received a call from Scottie's uncle that the authorities no longer called it a search, but rather a recovery as all four boys had drowned in the icy lake.

What follows is a narrative of the next two years of what became my search. My search for my son on the other side. It is currently 4:40am and I just concluded a meditation session that resulted in messages from my son through spirit writing.

At 1:45pm this afternoon I have a phone appointment with a world-famous medium Thomas John, to connect with Chris. So, although I finished writing this manuscript before Father's Day 2018 as I had promised Chris, my search for him and subsequent connection to him and his world continues. And it will continue until we are together on the other side.

Joe McQuillen
8/25/2018

CHAPTER ONE:

HIDE & SEEK

At 4:45 a.m. on May 2, 2017 I woke up hearing a familiar child's voice in my head saying, "hide again." Two days earlier, I had heard my wife describing to her brother how relentless our little boy Christopher was when he played hide and seek. As soon as you found him, he would take off for a new hiding spot, calling out "hide again" which came out "*hi gin*" in his excited two-year-old voice. He could have played that game forever.

After feeding the dog and making coffee I sat at my desk to write this book. It's a story of a journey back and forth from the other side. Tomorrow will mark 16 months since my boy crossed over after drowning in a Wisconsin lake, the result of a canoe accident that also took the lives of three of his friends. He was 21 at the time.

I can take myself back to that late afternoon early evening of January 3, 2016. There are police around, boats with lights on the lake, small groups of kids in shock and nearby, parents crying. I walk with an officer to the basement of the lake house to identify a picture. They wouldn't allow me to see my boy. But the photo was him. The clothes, the smile, the Celtic cross. It was him and not him at the same time. And my life would never ever be the same.

When Christopher crossed over he left, his adoring mother Sally, his 19-year-old sister Caroline, his 16-year-old brother

William and me, his father. He left his grandparents and many loving aunts, uncles, and cousins from both sides of the family. He left us (or so we thought) all in shock and broken hearted. He left friends, lots of friends, from Winnetka, from a boarding school in Tucson and college friends from Northern Illinois University (NIU).

One of the benefits of coming from a dysfunctional Irish family is that you really don't care a lot about what anybody out side of your family thinks. That pretty much holds true for most aspects of my life but not this book. I am not trying to convince you of anything; you have to get there by yourself. But I genuinely believe I can give hope and comfort to anyone who has experienced my kind of loss. I have told my story to other grieving parents and felt their relief at finding out that it is not over. The intense love of a parent hasn't died when his or her child has passed. I will use the terms crossing over and the other side going forward. And if these terms seem a bit "new age" to you, well, you'll come around.

I have always had an interest in the other side. I remember sitting with a friend at college who explained what it was like to have a medium for a mother. I was fascinated, and she was embarrassed. Her mom lived in Lily Dale, New York which was a center for mediums. I was intrigued but at age twenty, I had other distractions. Coincidentally, I later found that my classmate is a medium herself, living on a horse farm in Wisconsin.

After that, my only brush with a psychic occurred in the early 1980s. My sister Marcia and I were walking around DuPont Circle in Washington, DC and on a lark, we went for a tarot card reading. I was nervous as all get out. The woman said my current girlfriend was with her parents surrounded by water on three sides. She also told me that my girlfriend was there to decide about our relationship and that it wouldn't work out. At the time, my girlfriend was on Cape Cod at her parent's beach house and when she returned home to D.C., she did indeed end the relationship. Although I would like to have blamed the gods, I believe the decision was due to the fact that I was a horrible boyfriend. When my sister came out from her reading, she was disappointed. The reader told her she was going to be the mother of 12 children. Being a divorced, single working mom in her 40s, with two children, she dismissed the reading completely. As we walked toward Georgetown for lunch I asked her about her recent love interest. Wasn't he a widower with 10 kids? My sister and Tom were married within a few years and she did take on the role of mother for the younger girls. We were not trying to make our current events match the reading, but something was going on.

In 2001 or 2002, someone gave me the name of a medium. I was looking for answers to life's questions and thought I would see what a medium would say. We met in a conference room of a library and I'll admit I felt a little goofy sitting there with incense and candles. She told me that my parents and my grand-mother came through to her. She also told me my parents were not together on the other side, which has been confirmed by other mediums I've consulted. The reading was pretty general, and I was feeling disappointed. However, toward the end of the reading, she told me my Dad had a message to confirm it was indeed him. He was showing her a caboose and told her to say the word "railroad." This got my attention. I have always felt that every family has a unique culture. If your dad was a teacher, you were from a teacher's family. If he was a coach, the culture was coaching. We were a railroad family. My father retired after 40 years working on the railroad. My mother's father retired from the railroad, as did her brother, my adored Uncle Bill. There were five boys in my family, all of whom worked on the railroad at one time. I had myself been a brakeman on a caboose working with my father when I was a young man. As a kid I vividly remember spending the night at a railroad yard with my Dad. He was a yardmaster at the time and his office was atop an aluminum tower that resembled a water tower that overlooked the rail yard. It was probably the place I felt closest to him. You have to understand there was no way this woman could have known anything about my Dad. She only knew my first name and there was no Google at the time for her to search for details about my life. "Railroad" was the one thing that truly described us as a family. Holy cow! I was a convert, I believed.

At a follow-up visit, she also told me that my boy Chris was an Indigo Child. At the time, I didn't know what that term meant. She also told me he would be diagnosed as having A.D.D. She dismissed this diagnosis and told me it only meant that he *answered to a different dimension.* I used this phrase in my eulogy for Chris because he surely did.

Let me introduce myself, lest you think I am some kind of new age wack job. I am a 60-year old father of three (one on the other side). I have been happily married for 26 years. I am at heart a blue-collar kid from Buffalo New York. I spent a few years working on the railroad, a few years working in unions in D.C. and worked for more than 25 years in the car business in Chicago. I eventually became a partner in several dealerships until I sold out and entered the mortgage business in 2009. I have been more successful than I had any right to be. But I have also worked my tail off. I sport a crew cut, have a broken nose (that I secretly like) and still play hockey. I do however tell people that I'm on my last dog and my last pair of skates. I am also in recovery from alcohol for more than 31 years. I believe this has allowed me to find a connection with my God or Higher Power, which has assisted me in connecting with my son, Chris. My experience in recovery has led me to a belief in God. And Chris' death has brought me closer to him, though it didn't happen all at once. When Chris first passed I was angry at God. I would still hit my knees every night, but I wasn't shy about letting God know that I was pissed at Him for taking my son. It wasn't long before God let me know that he didn't take Chris (although he was happy he was home), but rather Chris' free will and recklessness caused him to pass early and cross over. God let me know that as a Father he cried with me and hurt with me, and held me close through the long lonely days and nights.

Maybe the best way to best introduce you to who Chris was is through his eulogy. I delivered it to a packed church after a wake the previous night attended by over 2000 people.

Thoreau said that "if a man does not keep pace with his companions perhaps it is because he hears a different drummer"

My Christopher heard that different drummer. When he was a kid and diagnosed with A.DD I sought some spiritual counsel and was told that just meant that Chris answered to a different dimension, and so he did.

Forgive me if I need to stop and compose myself, as I have inherited my father's sentimentality when it comes to my kids. And I so dearly love my Christopher.

It was never easy to hold on to Chris. Sally said it was like water slipping through your fingers. But my goodness he had an impact and you knew he had been there. Maybe just by the smile left on all of our faces. He was not an easy boy to get…. But once he took hold it was for good.

Although he was a quandary, some got him early. The lovely Miss B and vice principal Schaecher who would pick him up to insure he got to middle school. He didn't like school and wouldn't do homework… but this was the same kid, his teacher reported who would leave the classroom to help his friend administer insulin to help regulate his diabetes.

He wore Hawaiian shirts partied too much, and when he would come home he was sick and needed caring, (which his mom lovingly provided) and a large duffle bag full of dirty laundry. Most of which was not even familiar to us.

He lived life doing 90 mph in a 30-mph zone. He flipped a pickup truck en route to work at the ranch, fell down a 30 ft. mine shaft, hiked Peru with a fever equaling shock, and it never slowed him down.

And we knew despite our warnings and trepidation that it never would.

Somehow, we knew that we only had him for a short time… so we cherished every moment.

Life on life's terms was not something my boy ascribed to. It was life on Chris' terms. And if you wanted in you needed to accept that…it wasn't enabling it was just the terms of the contract. But you already know that, you have already been roped in, and you made the same deal, didn't you?

When a dear friend's mom passed, and he wanted to get back for the services, he packed his jeep and started home from Tucson (after a Western Union stop due to a lost atm card…but that was part of the deal too.)

Despite a long conversation regarding stopping resting, hotel stays and safe driving, he showed up 28 hours later in time for the wake. It was only 1,743 miles and he had something he needed to do. Answering to that different dimension. When his cousin was headed to wilderness he turned around after being back in Vermont one day and drove back 900 miles a mere 15 hours to accompany him. Of course, the backpack he borrowed unknown to him had a camping hatchet in a side pocket, and airport security had some concerns… part of the deal. He charmed his way through security and got his cousin safely to wilderness and returned home (less one hatchet). See what I mean… life on Chris' terms

We were worried about our boy and at 16 years old, we sent him to In Balance Ranch Academy in Arizona. There he finished high school and found himself. He stayed on after graduation as a life coach and worked with struggling teens for a year or so. He was happy and fulfilled and we had a peace we hadn't felt regarding him before, but he needed to answer that call again

We will be forever grateful to the entire Barrasso Family and Thad for giving us back our son. But he got you…he roped you in too, and then he was gone.

He found his way to NIU and a fraternal brother-hood of AKL. He found acceptance and love, and he was happy again. Although it all appeared like a scene out of Animal House, there was pure love and true loyalty in his daily life. And I am grateful for what was given back to him in kind. A year ago, after returning from a family cruise on Christmas, he announced that he needed to get back to the house as one of his brothers wasn't going home and would be alone for Christmas. He packed up a couple of plates of food, wrapped a gift and headed back to DeKalb. That was my son. Perhaps one of his finest moments at NIU was when he mentored a young man with special needs and they performed together in a talent show with his adoring mom in attendance.

My God he loved his mom…. from the first moment he appeared and the love both ways was fierce.

He loved and felt protective of his sister Caroline. When she suddenly returned home from college for a weekend, Chris left a formal and showed up (a little worse for wear) to be with her. He will always look out for her. He was in awe of the young man his little brother William had become. Looking at a photo over Christmas I commented that Will was cool. Oh man… he's twice as cool as I ever was…Will's the man he said. Chris' approval was something that came like a thief in the night but my God, we all longed for it.

He loved being Irish, the Buffalo Bills and being a McQuillen. When his cherished cousin Kerry passed away in February 2013 leaving two little boys, he announced he wasn't returning home but was staying in Buffalo to help out, because "that's what family does." He connected with Ryan and Big Al and roped you all in… life on Chris' terms.

One blessing for Sally, Caroline, William, and me was that the last month with him was pure joy. He was happy. He had his friends in DeKalb, his New Trier pals here and his family around him. All stepping to his beat. He ate, he drank, we spoiled him for Christmas (which he loved), shot pool, bowled, he clubbed and lived. And he knew he was adored.

The term beloved is overused in most eulogies but not in this case. Not for Christopher. He was beloved by his parents, grandparents, siblings, godparents, uncles, aunts, cousins, and his loving heartbroken friends… all of you, all of us. We made the deal on his terms... it was short. But you somehow knew it would be. Thank you for loving my Boy

I so dearly love my Chris. But he wasn't afraid to shoot an angle. So that Christmas night when he announced he was heading back to DeKalb to be with a friend left alone at Christmas, I jumped in to help. We packed a plate full of food and I ran to Walgreens for a gift. But I had a sneaky suspicion that the *friend* was a good-looking co-ed or a keg party. At the wake the friend from that Christmas at NIU pulled me aside with tears in his eyes to tell me the story. It was just as Chris presented. And then I met Daniel, the boy he mentored during the Penguin Players variety show. This is a theatre troop made up of young adults with emotional disabilities. Both boys wanted me to know, in their own way, how much they loved my Chris and how much he impacted their lives.

A year later on January 3, 2017, a day I assumed would be one of the most difficult since his passing. I received a call from one of Chris' college friends to tell me that a group of his friends were going to his grave at 2 p.m. and asked if I could join them. Since we had entertained eight or so of the kids on New Year's Day, before they headed back to DeKalb for college, we didn't expect them to return two days later to visit his grave. We were wrong. When I got to the grave I saw a few of Chris' dear pals and I broke out the hockey cooler filled with Chris' favorite beer. (Well, to be more accurate Stella was his favorite when I was buying and Landshark when he was). I also packed a few Sharps NA so I could toast the handful of friends I expected. Soon the circular drive at the cemetery began to fill up and his college friends began to emerge like the clown cars in the circus.

College kids were everywhere, hugging, kissing, and crying. My heart was singing. They were here to celebrate my boy. Then his childhood friends began to show up. I called Sally, Chris' mom, and told her she had to get to the grave right away. There were two dozen, kids in their twenties, in the cold of early January smoking cigars (mine of course) and toasting their beloved pal who had passed. But he hadn't passed, not really. Although he had crossed over, everyone there felt his presence, his love, and that very special Christopher thing. The celebration went on for more than three hours and still lives on in my heart. When I'm down I just close my eyes and I am amongst the gravestones with his friends. They are young, heartbroken and so full of love.

January 3, 2017

CHAPTER TWO:

THE LAKE IN WISCONSIN

Very early in the morning on January 3, 2016 I awoke with a feeling of dread. I had dreamt about missing a school assignment or some such nonsense. But I felt horrible. In a life full of near misses and close calls, this feeling was the worst one I can remember.

I couldn't shake it off, but I got out of bed to do what I normally do on a Sunday in the winter. I would get up, make coffee, feed the dog and do a little work before the noon kick-off of the Buffalo Bills game.

We have had a satellite dish since we moved to Winnetka in the summer of 1994, solely so that I could watch my hometown team. As my boys got older it became a tradition to watch the Bills' game together. When Chris was away at school he was able to watch online thru the NFL Sunday Ticket Package which allowed him to stream the game. When my oldest brother Jerry - who lived in Boston was alive - we would watch the game and call each other back and forth to discuss plays. You need to understand that we were raised around Sunday dinners at mom and dad's house, a pickup football game and then the Bills game. It was mandatory attendance and simply part of growing up.

When my mother passed in 1992, we actually moved her funeral service to accommodate the Bill's 1 p.m. kickoff. And she wouldn't have had it any other way. On the morning of her

21

funeral we had a pickup football game in Delaware Park followed by her funeral service at St. Mary's of the Lake Church and a reception/Bills game at my brother Paul's house for our family, neighbors and childhood friends. I didn't know then what it was, but I knew the somber feeling at the funeral was replaced with a spirit of mirth at Paul's home. It's only later (maybe now) that I understood it was my Mom's spirit working the room, loving that her family was gathered together remembering her.

That January 3, 2016 morning, I was waiting for Chris to arrive back from the house party in Wisconsin to watch the game with me. A little after noon, I got a call from his friend Scottie saying that Chris and three of his friends were missing. I asked him to text me the address as I pulled on a hunting jacket and boots and headed up north. I received the text with the address at 12:35 p.m. (I'm looking at it on my phone as I write) and half an hour later received a call from Scottie's uncle saying that it was now a recovery effort since they had found his body. Eventually the coroner would place the time of death between 3 a.m. and 4 a.m. that morning. That was the same time that I woke with the feeling of dread in my heart. Just recounting this now still brings me to tears.

There were so many plans to be made. And quickly. The phone calls to my sister Marcia, Chris' beloved godmother, and the rest of the family, were heart-wrenching. Michael, my best friend and Chris' godfather, flew back from a vacation in Florida the next day. Even though I was in a state of shock, I was trying to get everything done, somehow. Thank God for Michael. He stayed with me in those dark days. I had to bury my grief deep inside in order to get things done. I had to make funeral arrangements, choose a burial plot, and organize a reception.

I agreed to talk to the *Tribune*, because I wanted to share who Chris was. He wasn't a spoiled North Shore kid, but a sweet sensitive son and friend. The newspaper ran a nice story and a follow up one year later. I will be forever grateful to Duaa Eldeib, the staff writer, for her gentleness and sensitivity.

> http://www.chicagotribune.com/news/local/breaking/
> ct-wisconsin-canoe-accident-20160104-story.html

> http://www.chicagotribune.com/news/ct-north-shore-
> canoe-deaths-one-year-later-met-20170101-story.html

We buried Chris on January 8, 2016 at Sacred Heart cemetery. It's a beautiful spot with trees and a view of the sky. There is a black granite grave marker with the Buffalo Bills logo on the bottom right corner. This is a place for me to come and visit my boy. I keep a folding chair in my Jeep and always carry a lit cigar so Chris knows it's me. Some amazing things have happened there, things that have helped me ease into an awareness of life on the other side.

CHAPTER THREE:

THE JOURNEY

Here is where the search for Chris begins. I will explain how I first contacted Chris through mediums and then on my own. I have kept copious notes on each visit, whether they were with mediums on the phone, in person or in my own head during meditation. I write down the messages as they're given to me. I have not reviewed many of them since I originally wrote them until now.

Here is the definition of a medium according to *From Crossing Over to Connection* by Amanda Linette Meder:

> A medium is someone who stands at the midway point between two realms and acts as a conduit that transfers energy between those two points of contact. In the case of working with your deceased loved ones, a medium can transfer images, words, thoughts and emotions back and forth between the physical world (where you are) and the spirit world (where they are).

A few days after Chris' passing I contacted Nancine. She was the medium I had visited so many years ago with whom I had kept in touch. She had long ago moved from Illinois to Surprise, AZ, so I would have to speak to her by phone.

Here is what Nancine told me about the accident. "They were in the canoe horsing around when it capsized. The feeling of his lungs filling up with water was a new feeling and confusing. There was some panic but no pain or suffering. His spirit was pulled quickly from his body. His cousin Kerry, whose boys he nannied when she passed, was there to greet him. She pulled his spirit and helped him cross over. Seeing her surprised him. He was concerned and said to Kerry, "I don't get it."

He was filled with surprise and delight. There was color, sensation and beauty. "Dad, you gotta see this…it's fucking amazing!" He told Nancine that he was in my room after he passed to look in on me. He told me to notice my breath in the cold air because he will add a kiss.

Nancine said that he was in a period of attunement which means getting acclimated. She said that Chris told her there is wall of pure spirit. My brother Jerry, who had passed two years previously, greeted Chris and promised to keep a watchful eye on him. Jerry also sent a message that he loved the other side. My niece Kerry is working over there with young children who passed. Their souls are preparing to return.

Chris described being wrapped in a bubble wrap of pure love connecting to his hand (I have no idea what this means but it was in my notes, so you figure it out.) According to Nancine, Chris is surprised by it all. He is not afraid. He is all in…he is zooming… rejuvenated.

He told Nancine. "You get what you want …but you don't know what to do with it. If I take this can I still have that?" She also told me that Chris had an overwhelming desire to fix things for us. Nancine recommended that I use some humor with him. My humor is calming to Chris. He said he's not afraid but rather weirded out. Tell mom, "I am so sorry."

He told Nancine, "If I could have changed who I was for

the sake of my mom and dad, I would have. I most definitely picked you and mom. I'm very weirded out but I feel awesome. First time I felt awesome in a long time"

In the last part of his contact he told Nancine that he and I are from the same soul family, that he's dusting off the energy from his last moments on this side, and that I damn well better know he loves me. He requested a single white rose from me for his grave after the funeral, which he wasn't sure he was going to attend.

She ended simply with "he's happy." As heartbreaking as losing him was we took some solace that he was happy and feeling awesome. This was something that our sensitive boy struggled with on this side.

This was a lot for me: Losing my beloved son and then hearing from him on the other side was unsettling. My life and my priorities took a turn toward the world Chris now lived in. I wanted more.

The days and weeks that followed were a soft sad blur. We were all broken, and we were sleep walking through the days. We each carried our grief in our own way. But there were similarities. William and Sally turned inwardly while Caroline and I filled each waking hour with activity so as not to let the feelings overwhelm us. It was horrible. I couldn't take away my pain, much less fix theirs, despite how much I loved them. It was as if I was an amputee waking up each morning forgetting about my loss until the reality swept over and you know you're not whole and will never be again. But if I can just hold on long enough to hear from Chris…one more day, one more week…

My next reading with Nancine on the phone was March 3, just about two months after Chris' passing. I was barely holding on emotionally and couldn't wait to be in contact with Chris again. The funeral had long passed, and the reality of his crossing was hitting home. I needed that contact and I got it.

Nancine said that he was referring to me as Dad, but also by another name. She asked me if he had ever called me Pap or Pip? I told her he often called me Pop or Pops. Yes, she said that's what he's calling you. He told her he was getting adjusted and everything moved fast. "Dad, this is fast."

She said he was showing her that we used to roll our eyes together and had the ability to share a laugh. She said he hopes I will still do that.

She told me he had some regrets. He didn't feel that he had been as successful as he had wanted. He should have gone to a trade school to build things. That's what he's doing now. Check out the constellations, he said. It's a breeze. He loves it. He was impressed with me and my success, he told her. Boot strap attitude, he wanted to be more like me. He's happy now and he's got what he wanted.

He wanted his mom to know that he was in love before he crossed. It was important that she knew this. I assumed he was referring to a recent heartbreak he experienced at NIU but Nancine insisted that it was about a local girl from our town or the next one over. She insisted that the name started with a hard C or K. The relationship never moved beyond a close friendship because neither one was ready and didn't want to risk what they had. He said he never told us because he didn't even know. He said, "It's enough to know that, just natural Pop." Sally shared this message with Claire Clark, the lovely girl from the next town over, who had been close friends with Chris since they were kids.

Nancine said Chris told her that life was a struggle for him on earth and there were things he couldn't do due to anxiety. He always would say, "Let me do this, when in truth I always needed help."

He told me that the other side is like a video game. Everything changes suddenly. The journey is fun. There were colors and sounds beyond a roller coaster. He said he always thought he was a loner but there are three dudes and a woman who have always been with him," Nancine said. We call them Angels.

I needed to know about his last moments on earth. Sally and I were tortured at the thought of him drowning in that frigid cold Wisconsin lake. "I didn't feel a lot, Pop. I think it was because I was starting to become spirit. It was like falling over in a crowd." He was talking about an aunt (on whom he used to play jokes) meeting him. This was his Aunt Pat who passed away the previous August. "By the way…about the jokes, she knows now." He was met by family pets who calmed him down.

Nancine said he was becoming contemplative. "On our side he always felt like a screw up" and even now he is terribly sorry that the accident and his recklessness causes us such grief. He is remembering Mom bringing him along to the grocery or little trips around town. He used to take a stuffed animal around with him. "Mom will remember…she will know it's me and I love her so much."

Chris said the other side is 100% love. There is no judgement and lots of guidance. He enjoys the learning and has no worries. He says he needs to grow and move forward.

He said he sees that his sister is in love. "Pop, she's in love. It will be okay; she could do a lot better." He thinks she is working too hard to keep it going. Chris thinks relationships should be a "lot like you and mom's."

I asked him if he woke me up between 3 a.m. and 4 a.m. on January 3. "Absolutely, I left my body and stopped by what was familiar." He was out of his body. Chris said at some point in the journey he possibly had an opportunity to go back. He said he didn't choose one or the other; he got distracted and then it was too late.

He said all three boys who passed with him are okay. One had a harder time crossing over but he's fine now.

I will talk later on about his drowning. But the answers from the other side have all been the same. It was peaceful and painless. Sally and I both thank God for that.

Chris said he wanted to give us more about the funeral ceremony. He did in fact attend. He said he was in the third row on the left side studying the people. He said he spent a lot of time by the flowers. He let Nancine know he loved flowers and was no longer ashamed to admit it. He acknowledged that great things were said about him and he was a little embarrassed and humbled. He wasn't sure he had filled the shoes in the way we spoke of him that day.

He made references to his grave and said he likes to stop there. He mentioned a big tree near his grave and that I should take a load off.

He told Nancine that we loved him to a fault. He was reckless and felt he could push the envelope because he knew he had both of us in his corner. He did not know he was going early. He thought there would be a lot more weddings. He loved celebrations. His birthday was coming up and Caroline's was soon after that. He said we should focus on hers as she felt it was too soon to ask for any attention. I can report that that is no longer the case and we shower our sweet 21-year-old daughter with loving attention, and there is hell to pay when we fail to do that.

He spoke to Nancine about his cousin Kerry who passed at age 43 leaving two beautiful adopted boys behind. She will come up in future readings by mediums always referring to her by name. He said he liked my brother Jerry a lot. He wanted me to know that although they are together I shouldn't worry because, "No way will I replace you with Jerry." That comment was made because Jerry was my oldest brother and since I was the youngest of ten, he absolutely adored me and I knew it. He said Jerry is a fun spirit and is very popular. Jerry promised to let me know that Chris was okay.

Wrapping the session up, Nancine said that Chris is happy and peaceful at what he accomplished by coming through. He had tears of joy because, "I got through to my dad."

Nancine told me Chris could feel my touch and that he liked it when I kiss his picture. I do that often; I have a copy of his photo on my dashboard, and mounted pictures on the wall leading upstairs. She said he has a cute smile especially for his mother.

Then he was gone......

It's probably time to introduce you to Chris' mother. The moment I laid eyes on her in the summer of 1988 I knew she was the one. I wasn't yet ready to settle down, and neither was she, but I couldn't ignore the chemistry. She was pretty, blond, and so full of life. She wore coveralls and purple Naf Naf high top sneakers that looked like Chuck Taylor's Converse to me. My goose was cooked. We were engaged in 1990 and married on June 29, 1991. Our Christopher was born on April 15, 1994. The connection between Chris and his mom was immediate and intense. I was a spectator to this bond since there was only room for two in this love affair. But thankfully, I was invited in later on. Chris was such a gift. I have never seen one person make another one so whole. But that was their connection and that's their story. I will be telling you a lot about my loss because sometimes thinking about Sally's loss as a mom is unbearable. But I want you to know I'm aware of it. And I want her to know I know it.

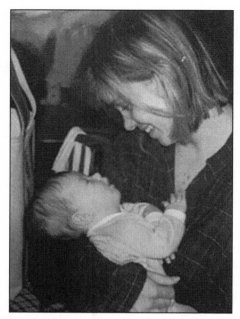

Early in March that year, Sally through a friend (thanks, Janet) flew to Denver for an intimate circle with Rebecca Rosen, a world renowned medium. It was a small group reading where everyone (at least everyone who had a crossed spirit step forward) would get a reading. Although this was Sally's reading, I was impatiently awaiting the result of the contact. To Sally's surprise the first spirit to come through was my brother Jerry. Rebecca said that Jerry was somehow a brother and a father figure. That is what he was to me. Rebecca was attempting to finish with another client in the intimate circle and was trying to have Jerry wait his turn. She obviously didn't know Jerry. I could hear her on the recording saying, "Okay, Jerry sit tight. We will get to you." But Jerry couldn't be put off in the afterlife any more than he could on this side.

Rebecca relented and Jerry came through. He wanted us to know that he was okay and that he made it. She said he was a very powerful soul, which would surprise no one. He said he had nine siblings. "Tell my brother I'm with the others; he's with Bobby (who crossed in 1977) and he's happy to see him again. My mother came through. Rebecca asked, "Who has a mother figure name Rita?" I think at this point my patient wife was getting tired of hearing from pushy McQuillen spirits. My mom said she was watching over Chris, and my sister Pat who had passed only a year before also made her presence known. She said they were in a group in heaven.

Sally's dad came through, which he will do in all of her subsequent readings. She said Warren loved to hunt which he did on earth and that was his heaven.

Finally, Chris came through for his momma. Since he was a new spirit, it was remarkable how clear he came through. Chris stated that he owned his death. It was a stupid choice to go in the canoe. It was an accident that was related to the drinking.

He said we were healing now and happy, which he indicated by jumping up and down. He's okay. He stated he loved the songs at the funeral and that he's glad you brought his scarf. He said he loves you asking for him and loves the tattoo. He was telling his mom he didn't linger and had no fear. The way he came into the world was the way he left. He didn't suffer. Rebecca said that Chris was showing his mom a Reese's Peanut Butter Cup. Unbeknownst to me until she explained it, Sally knew it was his favorite candy and would send him a bag of Reese's Peanut Butter Cups in the mail on special occasions or just as an I love you. Chris was sending it back. Rebecca confirmed that he was pretty happy, and that our dog Cassidy sees his spirit.

At this point not only did I know that there was another side, I knew that my boy was there and finding a way to communicate with us. I knew that I needed to find a way to build a bridge to his world so that we could communicate clearly and more often. There was never any place I would rather be that with my boy so learning how to break through to the other side was just a small detail. I missed him far too much.

My next reading was a phone reading with Nancine, my medium from so long ago, on May 26, 2016

He started by saying, "Tell Pop I'm sorry I'm late." She said Chis has been spending time with my mother, his grandmother who he never met. She is showing him family moments through what she could best describe as a view finder. Chris said that his mom and I should listen to the music he's giving back to us --in the rain, wind and lightning.

I asked Nancine to find out if I was dreaming the night he crossed. He said, "No, you weren't dreaming." It was an attempt to raise me up. "It's something that is really only understandable on our side." No worries he said. Trust me on this. He refers to a blue shirt or jacket. This keeps coming up in future readings.

We are pretty sure it was a Blue Buffalo Bills Jacket that was a Christmas gift from his godmother, Marcia.

He said I will be hearing him as if someone is calling me, "It's me." He told Nancine he walks with me. He is acknowledging the writing and performing of songs for him, but he prefers if people don't grieve too much. He wants us to know he acknowledges the grave and thinks it's amazing.

When I'm approaching the grave Chris said I should walk toward the tree. "I'm there."

Chris stated that August 15 was some sort of milestone for him on the other side. He said I should have a cigar to commemorate. "It's a big deal."

Nancine said Chris keeps sharing a concern about how sad we're feeling. He knows I am doing the best I can, but he warned me about leading my own life, not his. He also hopes his friends will live every moment fully.

Chris said his sister Caroline was doing alright but her grief was deep and quiet. She was doing her best to not let her grief cause her mother and me more pain. He wants me to keep an eye on his little brother Will. He said he will too. "Will needs to get his focus back on himself."

I asked Nancine what Chris misses. And she said he misses *words*. He wants me to bring him more instrumentals. Vibrations and sound therapy are how he communicates.

He said he was awed by how his mom pushed through her own depressing moments. Nancine said he was clapping for his mom. "Way to go. Fake it till you make it"

He told me to applaud his mom more as we walk this path. "Mom needs more applause. She is a bright star in other's lives. She is so gentle, she opens her heart, she's like me."

"Not that you don't have a nice smile dad, but mom has a great smile."

Nancine said Chris is referring to the view master again and my mom. He's chuckling while looking at stuff from my childhood. He cherishes them. He laughs because he sees that I was frustrated by small things when I was young. "I'm not the only one," he says.

At this point I had written some questions I wanted Nancine to ask him. I asked many, but I have only included the ones he chose to answer.

Q Where did mommy and I ever come up short?

A "You are short pop, but you never came up short." (He's funny, Nancie interjected.) Are you kidding me? He told her he wished he said thank you more often. He said he'll send a sign by a balloon.

Q Do you look forward to someday meeting me on the other side?

A Are you sure that's what you want Pop? There's plenty of time to plan. (He showed Nancine a hand shake, indicating it was a deal.)

Q I go to your grave often to connect. Do you meet me there? What do you think of it? What can I do to facilitate hearing from you?

A He laughs, "It's so you pop." He said I have to be willing to feel his energy. It's best to carve out a time regularly to feel his energy.

I asked Nancine to ask him about his brother and sister.

WILL

Things are being held in. Secretly Will is being swallowed up by a memory. Will shuts himself down and is afraid to surpass Chris. Chris told Nancine to tell me that he will handle it.

CAROLINE

"My gosh you are a grown woman...let it go." Chris says Caroline keeps asking, "What will I do without you?" Chris answers, "The same as you always did."

Chris is making an analogy about a small tree not needing support. He still doesn't like her boyfriend. (Ex by now. He's winking as if he'll handle this too. I guess he did.).

Nancine said he wants us to know he's doing the best he can. He heard Sally singing the song we wrote, "Take Care of my Baby." He was remembering when she would sing to him when he was a baby. He cherishes the song and "my sweet mom." He will send the song through vibrations to her.

He mentioned that he was worried about his friend Mish but trusted she would be okay.

He loves seeing his name. His roommate Raul put his name in lights. Very cool. But he wants everyone to remember their own names during this. But it is amazing. It reminds him of all the good he did.

He acknowledges the charity and goodwill done in his name (at this point it was only the funeral donations) so I guess he knew what was coming. "I don't know if I deserve it, but it pumps me up." But a warning to his dad "Don't pressure anyone." I promised him I would only press a little.

About August 15 being significant, Chris is advancing with energy and light. "I am having a ball…sitting on a rocket. Except for Gram (my mom), everyone is slower than me." Gramma is showing him about me. Ornaments of a parent's life. Chris is working with children on the other side."

"Raphael & Michael… God is the wind the seas and the stars. Chris is asking for the energy of Mary of Nazareth to be with his mom.

Chris tells Nancine that Bompa is watching him. Chris says it's a little irritating like when we would check in on him as a kid. Bompa is Sally's grandfather who died when Chris was almost four. Chris said he checks in all the time. Chris calls him "the Dude." He has been in the light a long time. He knows the ropes in heaven. Chris knows he is his great grandfather whom he didn't really know. He knows he's from his mother's side of the family, not connected to my mom.

In closing, Chris wants us to get more buoyant in grief. Like a fishing bobber. He wants me to feel him more and open my eyes and know that's he's there. Ask the angels for help here. "Get used to the signals and signs I'm limited to." He needs me to trust more. He shares my frustration, "We'll work on it together," he tells me. He will see me Sunday at his grave.

I ask Nancine to help me to hug him. "We don't need Nancy to hug," Chris told me. "Nancine, Chris," my medium said. "My name is Nancine,"

At this point I closed my eyes and crossed my arms (left over right) embracing my son. I felt his embrace in return and began to cry with relief. My boy was still here, and he still loved his old man.

What follows is an email from me and the response from Nancine. God Bless you, Nancine and thank you for lighting the way for me.

From: Joe McQuillen
Sent: Saturday, May 28, 2016 1:37 PM

Nancine,
Thanks for bringing Christopher to me. Do you see him
as well as hear him?

Hugging him when you signed off was very healing.
We did hug intensely at times.

I had a restless night and feel he may has visited me
as I requested. Can you confirm that?

Warmest Regards
Joe

Q1: Yes – both; it is called "clairvoyant (see)" and "clairaudient" (hear). I'm pretty sure I have explained however that the
"power to send the vision" is in the hands of the deceased.
For example, he was somewhat "fixed" on the blue jacket or
shirt during your last visit—something he apparently liked
(or likes) very much. Sweet Ones as I call those deceased
are pure light and energy but do present themselves with
what appears to be physical attire so we may in fact "see"
them and/or be certain. They are also renewed in spiritual
prowess and enjoy the ability to be mercurial in presence.
Your Christopher is somewhat "theatrical" and you may
expect "many hats" as he continues to enjoy his New Journey.

Q2: Yes, absolutely, Christopher is trying to visit you as you
ask. He likely wanted to know how the hug went at your end
inasmuch as you are each trying to work at "crossing over" to
the other step by step. He is in that new stage of innocence
and probably thinks you can easily cross over and see things

at "his place. "This is called: astral traveling and its okay
to engage so long as, once again, you make an intention to
"travel safely" and "return safely." Just ask Archangel Michael
and your guardian angels to protect and guide you in any
travel while you sleep.

You're doing a great job, Joe!
Angel Blessings,

Well…… that happened. I need to take a moment to reflect on
this spiritual travelogue. This last contact was on May 26, 2016.
It is less than five months since my son crossed. Five months is
the equivalent of a school semester. I've been known to learn
absolutely nothing in an entire semester even if I was already
familiar with the subject. Now I am running head first into a world
that I thought may have existed but had little bearing on my life.

This world was now every bit as important to me as the one
I live in. Because Nancine lived in Arizona these readings were
done on the phone. Although this emergence into Chris' world
was amazing, it wasn't enough. I wanted more. I had started
reading about the other side. I started downloading audio books
and listening to them in my jeep. One of the first books I read
was *From Crossing Over to Connection A Guide to Life after Death* by
Amanda Linett Meder. I stumbled on this book and I downloaded
and read it. It was a very clear and concise guide to life on the
other side. It provided me a glimpse of the world my boy was
now living in and his trip to get there. It brought me comfort
and allowed me to understand that all the pain in this situation
was about me. I was hurting, I was missing him, I felt a loss. He
was soul deep in what I envisioned was a warm tropical vacation
that didn't have to end.

CHAPTER FOUR:

THIS SUCKS....

Let me take a moment to explain that my journey to the other side in search of Chris has been nothing short of amazing. I have been given indisputable evidence that he is not only okay, but his spirit is often with me. He's there when I golf, when I drive in my jeep and when I sit at his grave in conversation with him. He has sent me signs and has played me songs to let me know he's around. But you need to know that none of that can repair the hole in my heart. None of it can equal a hug, a smile or an "I love you too, Dad." I have come away from encounters and readings feeling a great knowing we are still together in spirit. However, there is always the eventual deflating feeling that follows. Having his spirit is all I've got but please understand that it's not the same and will never be, until we are together on the other side.

I need to talk about Chris' grave and grave stone. The day after he passed, his godfather Michael and I began to organize all the arrangements for his funeral. After meeting with Grace Donnellan Martinsen, the funeral director, who was truly amazing (amazing grace ...get it), we worked out the details of waking and burying my beloved boy, whose body was en-route from Wisconsin. We needed a grave. Grace recommended Sacred Heart cemetery which was a mere three miles away. It was a typically cold and gray January day in the Chicago suburbs.

When we approached the woman from Sacred Heart (she was not anxious to deal with the cold), she got out of the car and showed us what options we had as we all looked over the snow-covered grave yard. She showed us a row of six plots that were available in the mostly sold out cemetery. Michael and I decided to take all six. We would work out the details later. She asked me where we wanted Chris buried in the row and I chose a spot on the end near a little tree. With that decision made, we moved on to the next of the many details.

On January 8, my son Chris was buried in the plot we picked. He requested I place one single rose on his grave in a reading, and as usual I did what he asked of me. Friends and family gathered, and a lone bagpiper played Danny Boy. Because it was winter the gravestone could not be placed until the frozen ground would be soft enough. So, getting the stone could be pushed down the list.

Over the next few weeks I would visit his fresh grave at the snow-covered cemetery. I was looking forward to the time when the weather would be mild enough to open a folding chair to sit next to and visit with my son and have a cigar. When the hawk finally stopped blowing in early March and a warm breeze covered the north shore I headed to Chris' grave. What I saw broke my heart. Unbeknownst to us, my son's grave was placed right next to the graves of a married couple, the Sheridans, who I've since learned are lovely people. However, with five empty plots to the north of his, Chris' grave location made it appear that he was the Sheridan's boy. I was pissed. I called Ascension Cemetery and spoke to the stuttering dingbat who never told us that we were placing Chris next to the Sheridan's plots. I asked her to speak to her manager and Bill Metz came on the line. Once I was calm enough to make myself understood, I explained that I wanted my son moved pronto. Bill said he would call me back. The next day he said that he went to the board and that they would reintern

Chris to one of the other plots for a 50% fee. I told Bill to go back to the board and see if they wanted to be forever described by me as the generous compassionate people of Ascension or the heartless bastards who imposed a 50% surcharge to fix their error.... I wrote the check. But I do refer to them as described as often as possible. (Side joke...do you know what Irish Alzheimer's is? It's where you forget everything but the grudges.)

In April, Chris' casket was moved one space north. After much soul searching I decided I would occupy the plot from where Chris had been moved since I couldn't bear anyone else in that spot. His mom will rest in the spot north of Chris'. This means our beautiful boy is between us. I wrestled with the decision whether to move him or not. I thought and prayed a lot (I swore a little also, maybe a little more than a little). The decision to move Chris was absolutely the right one. I often spend time there, and it needed to be just as it is. Later when I asked Chris, through Nancine, what he thought about the whole grave rotation, he laughed and said, "That's so you, pop." He also wanted me to know that the Sheridans "are not bad people."

The same day his casket was moved his gravestone was placed at the head. It is black granite with a Celtic Cross and the logo of his beloved Buffalo Bills on the bottom right.

CHAPTER FIVE:

IN PERSON...SORT OF

I was so grateful for the contact I had received, yet my soul needed more. I'm not even sure I knew what more meant, but I had to find it. This seeking led me to search for mediums online. I was drawn to a name and sent an email. I then went about working on deals. Soon, I received a call on my cell. I remember very clearly walking into a small conference room for privacy. Andrew Anderson was calling me back about scheduling a session. Let's book it. I can always cancel later. I had booked a session for Thursday noon at his house in the western suburbs about 40 minutes from my home.

Recently I had ordered some shamrock seeds. I wanted to plant them in the loose dirt around Chris' grave. I figured I could plant them in the morning before my appointment with Andrew. I had started keeping a carry bag in the back of the Jeep with a trowel, some sheers, a golf towel and granite cleaner. I wanted the grave to be perfect for Chris and for me. I would also keep a folding chair, so I could sit next to him and light a cigar, so he would know it was me and chat. Originally the folding chair had a maple leaf on it because I picked it up on our annual family reunion in Crystal Beach, Ontario. I replaced that worn chair with a Buffalo Bills chair. Sitting next to Chris reminded me of when he fell down a mine shaft while hiking in northern Arizona.

Yeah that happened. After graduating high school at In Balance Ranch academy near Tucson, he stayed on at the school as a life coach. In the fall of 2012, Chris was assisting a staff guide taking kids hiking and pool jumping in Havasupai. The leader had a lapse in judgement and had the kids walk into a cave. Chris fell down 25 feet in an abandoned shaft and landed on a ledge. Until the call came on January 3 about Chris being missing, the time between the first call from the ranch when they told me Chris had fallen, and the second call that said he was on a helicopter headed to Flagstaff was the longest 45 minutes of my life. When I asked during the first call about possible paralysis, I was told if they airlifted him to Las Vegas it was because of paralysis, if Flagstaff then he wasn't paralyzed. He was airlifted out and taken to Flagstaff hospital. I got the call and starting balling in relief. I called my dear pal Mike Sawyer and he immediately drove three hours from Scottsdale to Flagstaff. The initial plan was for Mike to bring Chris to his house to recover for a few days and then fly him home to his mom and me. When Mike got to the hospital, things were chaotic, and Chris was a mess. To Mike it felt more like a M*A*S*H* unit than a hospital. When Mike told the doctor, he was taking Chris with him, the doctor explained that he didn't have the authorization. Mike replied that he was leaving with my boy one way or the other and that the doctor had better decide to get out of the way or get run over. It didn't hurt that two strapping ranch classmates of Chris were holding the door and glowering at the doctor. While driving back south, Mike, who had experience in sports management, called the Phoenix Suns' orthopedic doctor who was vacationing in Europe. Arrangements were made for Chris to be checked into Scottsdale Osborne hospital, where Mike and his family stayed with him through the night and the first of two surgeries until I was able to get there. I was there when Chris woke from the second surgery. From that point on my Christopher called him Uncle Mike, a title until that time, was reserved only for Michael, his godfather.

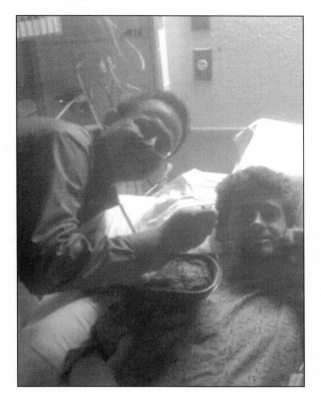

The wonderful staff at Scottsdale Osborne let me settle in next to my boy in an easy chair and I stayed with him that way for the better part of a week. His uncle Mike Sawyer brought Chinese food on one night and not to be outdone, his Uncle Mike Holmberg had Fleming Steak House cater a dinner. I sat next to Chris on his left side and reveled in appreciation that my boy was safe, alive and safe. We watched movies and he slept, and I basked in the love we had for each other. One moment that continues to sustain me when the grief is overwhelming that I recall is that during the first evening when we were alone, Chris reached over and took my right hand held it on his chest. The world stopped moving for that long moment, and at times I wished it never restarted.

I will sit next to his grave just like when we were in Scottsdale and I will talk to him. I do that, pretty often actually. I look out through the hedges at the back of the cemetery and envision how Chris would look when he was coming through the glass security gate at the airport when he came home for a visit. A duffle bag in his hand and a smile on his face. When I meditate at his grave I imagine him walking through the hedges, and I know he can see me. The day of my first visit with Andrew I straightened the area around the grave and planted shamrocks. They actually took root and even now a full season later you can see them. On this visit to the grave I told Chris I was heading off to see a guy named Andrew and would appreciate it if he could make time for the old man and come through. Chris didn't disappoint.

When I made the appointment, Andrew told me to bring pictures of the person I wanted to contact. I had one of my parents and a handful of my Christopher, smiling and so full of love and life.

This is the first time I'm reviewing these notes since the session, and I must admit that I'm amazed all over again. If the first session with a medium is as amazing as this one, the ones that follow are fulfilling but lack a bit of the initial wonder. Remember I was on pins and needles hoping to contact my beloved son with a medium in person. That's what I was hoping for, but I knew that I could also be really disappointed after the session.

Andrew, a man in his mid-forties, escorted me to his office. It was a little awkward and I thought he seemed a bit aloof. We sat in a small airy yet warm office. His desk was full of the normal medium accoutrements. Sage, candles, crystals and rocks. The framed posters on the wall were soothing and I wondered if there was a catalog or website all the mediums ordered from or was there a cosmic decorator. Maybe, I'll ask later.

So, at noon on June 30, 2016, almost six months since Chris crossed over, I walked into my appointment with my son. I was listening to a book by George Anderson and a mother was describing the feeling of walking into a medium for the first reading. You are so excited and so afraid that you will leave with no contact. If it has ever happened to you (it did once for me) it's hard to describe the empty feeling that settles into your heart. When nothing in the world matters more at that moment than contacting your loved one, a swing and a miss is gut wrenching. All of this nervousness was going on as I sat in front of Andrew. He asked me for the photos I had brought to the reading.

Andrew held a large crystal that he turned in one hand as squinted over my shoulder. He told me the other side is beautiful and peaceful with amazing colors and love. He said my Dad was coming through. He said my dad had an alcohol problem and had a tough life.

My Dad said he loved me very much. And although he did his best to show it (he did, and I adored my Dad) he wished we had the same type of relationship that Chris and I had. Andrew reported that although my mom was also over there, they don't stay together on the other side. (Why do mediums have to keep rubbing that in?) They came together for this reading and come together for family occasions. Andrew said they indicated that they were all together for a very recent occasion. I told him that the day before was my 25the wedding anniversary. Andrew confirmed that was it. My father was very proud of the man that I had become. And Andrew said they indicated that I have had more than my measure of success. They were both very proud and Andrew said "no offense" but my success was a pleasant surprise to them. He said my Mom feels bad she didn't have more time. My Dad passed away in 1988 and he had lived long enough to see me sober and embarking on a career. My mom saw me married and settled down. I know I felt her spirit around the nursery when my kids were babies.

Andrew now looked over my shoulder and said Chris was coming through. Andrew is clairvoyant as well as clairaudient. That means he can see Chris as well as hear him. He described that seeing him was like looking through pea soup. Andrew started in right away. He said Chris acknowledges I was wearing a bracelet he gave me and is aware I had just planted something for him. Before I left the house, I pulled out a leather bracelet with the Disney Character Goofy on the clasp. Chris had picked it out and gave it to me in Disneyworld when he was five or six. And that morning prior to driving to Andrew's, I stopped by his grave and planted shamrock seeds around the loose dirt on the bottom of his grave. Chris also wanted to acknowledge the blue jacket. This item had been mentioned by Nancine. It had to be the reversible blue Bills jacket that was a Christmas gift from his beloved godmother Marcia. Well, I thought, "better buckle up" because this shit is real. Chris also acknowledged that we celebrated his birthday on April 15 with balloons. Andrew pointed to a poster (probably from the psychic website) with hundreds of Chinese lanterns floating in the sky. He said Chris was pleased that we celebrated his birthday just the way we always did. And we did. On Chris' birthday, Sally, Caroline, William and I did our family birthday thing. On the kids' birthdays we have a special and not inexpensive dinner at Ron of Japan. And although it was very bittersweet, there was no way we wouldn't celebrate Chris' birthday in our special way. After dinner, we went to Duke Childs PlayFields (after giving up on the wind-swept Tower Road

Beach) where we released Chinese lanterns into the sky up to our beloved Christopher.

You have to understand that we were only about 15 minutes into my session. Everything Andrew brought up was spot on. He even described Christopher's looks and his very sweet and irreverent personality. There was not even one moment where I had to stop and try to connect the dots. Not one *"I don't get it moment."* Chris said he was very sorry. It was just a stupid accident. Andrew stated that he repeated that a number of times. He said it wasn't even his idea that he was following not leading. He said Chris didn't suffer and it was like passing out. Andrew indicated that the high alcohol content helped facilitate this. Chris said that his cousin Kerry greeted him. This comment is consistent with all mediums I have talked to before and after this session. Andrew said that Chris came through holding a little girl's hand stating that she was his sister. In 1998, before conceiving William, Sally miscarried. She was certain that it was a girl. We now know that this baby is with Chris on the other side. Andrew said that Chris is very funny and loved. Andrew, who's pretty straight-laced, asked me if Chris swears a lot. This made me smile and certainly reinforced that he was talking to the right spirit. Andrew said he is very funny and, "...as a matter of fact he is making fun of your haircut...and oh yeah...he curses a lot." Andrew told us that Chris always knew how much we loved him but admits he took it for granted. He doesn't now. Chris said we couldn't have been better parents or loved him more.

Chris mentioned that the entire family came together on the other side to celebrate our wedding anniversary the day before. Andrew asked me how many siblings I had left on this side as the group on the other side was rather large yesterday. (As a kid you should have seen the looks on the terrified restaurant hosts face when we all went for a fish fry...table for how many?)

I told Andrew I had four siblings on this side. Andrew told me no, I only had one. I had to pause to think. The fates and a tragic car wreck in December 1956 blended two families of cousins into one. Although we were all raised as brothers and sisters, Marcia was my only blood sister left on this side. Andrew wasn't probing or guessing; he was stating this fact.

Andrew looked at one of the pictures I had brought, with my Chris smiling and engaging in some joyful activity. He said that there was another side of Chris. Sad and depressed. Sometimes he didn't even want to be here. We knew that. We knew that we passed on depression and alcoholism genetically to our son. So, it was very important for us to know that what happened was just a stupid accident.

I guess I need to recount the events of Jan 2 and 3 of 2016. Chris had decided to join his pals at his friend's parents' beach house on Lake Beulah, just across the border in Wisconsin. Although I was always worried about the herd mentality around drinking, especially with this group, we had hoped that the rural environment would be safer than celebrating the last day of vacation in Chicago. As people had reported, the drinking started at a local bar and continued back at the beach house. Around 3 a.m. Chris and three boys went outside to get high. They passed the unlocked boat house and decided to go on a canoe ride. Four boys jumped into a three-man canoe without life jackets. They decided as a group to leave their cell phones in the boat house so as not to lose them or get them wet. We can only presume that they were roughhousing as usual and that the canoe overturned. Although they were only in about ten feet of water, they were dressed in layered clothing and heavy Timberland boots. (they all wore Timberland boots they called Tim's) The frigid water and ice encrusted shoreline added to the catastrophe. When the hungover friends woke in the morning they couldn't find the four boys. Looking out over the lake someone saw a capsized canoe, and eventually someone called the authorities.

Andrew told me Chris is very happy. He told me Chris was an old soul and had many lives and is now done. He's staying on the other side. He told Andrew that he sits on the end of my bed. He comes with me to his grave but would have preferred to be cremated.

Andrew felt Chris was a pretty advanced spirit. Andrew said Chris was at that moment laughing at my gray hair. He said that his cousin Kerry and her mom, his aunt Pat, are there. Andrew asked me, "I have never used this word in a reading about souls on the other side, but do they bicker a lot?" I smiled and said they were famous for bickering when they were together. "They are still doing it," said Andrew. This made me smile, as I knew Chris was with McQuillens and that they would be looking out for him. Nobody circled the wagons like the McQuillens, in this world or the next. Chris acknowledged *the star* and only now, writing this did I put together that his Uncle Charlie, Sally's brother, had purchase a star and named it after him after his crossing. He also wants us to know he is with Casey. Casey, our beloved Lab who lived for 14 years, is over there with Chris. She was about six months old when we brought Chris home from the hospital. Sometimes we wondered if Casey thought Chris was her son. When it was time to put Casey down when her body was failing her, Chris would not allow us to do it without him. Sally, Chris and I held Casey as she crossed over, and apparently, she was waiting for her Christopher to follow.

Chris mentioned his dear friend Mish from NIU. He would simply state that she was his best friend. Although they were the same age, she couldn't help mothering my boy when Sally was not around. We asked Mish to do a reading at the funeral and we adore her. Andrew said that although they were not romantically linked on this side, they had been married in a past life. Chris told Andrew that Mish was becoming a daughter to us. Andrew was amazed at how much of the world Chris had seen. He was mentioning Utah, where he spent 45 days in wilderness at the beginning of his journey in recovery. He told Andrew, "Tell mom I hear every word" and that he is "so sorry" that he caused us so much pain. Andrew said he's golfing up there, something we would do together, and I always feel him when I'm golfing. He repeated that Chris swears a lot and that he is funny. He keeps everyone laughing on the other side, just the way he did on this side.

Andrew said Chris knew how we felt, that we never got enough of him. It always seemed that just when he arrived somewhere it was always too soon time to go. Chris said he is now around us all the time. "You asked for it, "he said smiling, "Now you got it." Then the timer bell rang, and my time was up. I assumed Chris knew that because he seemed to be wrapping up in anticipation. This was amazing. I was actually hearing from Christopher from the other side. Not only that, I could look into someone's face as he spoke to and heard back from my boy. Only much later was I able to grasp that passing over is like walking from one room to another. The energy or spirit isn't gone. My boy wasn't gone. This event was going to take some processing, but for now I just wanted to get in my jeep, light a cigar and listen to a Jimmy Buffett tune knowing Chris was along for the ride.

Jimmy Buffett has always been important to both Chris and I. Jimmy's music always connected us. I'm including a true story about Jimmy Buffet and Chris, with me comfortably on the sidelines that I will now share with you....

My son Christopher attended his first Jimmy Buffett concert when he was four years -old. Don't Stop the Carnival was full of music, whistles and colored beach balls flying through the air, and he was hooked. On and off over the years Chris and I would hit one of Jimmy's summer dates in Chicago. Jimmy was my favorite musician, but I never attempted to influence Chris with regards to musical preference. Yet he took to Jimmy the same way he took to wearing the Hawaiian style shirts that I sported since my 20s. (Who would have guessed that Tommy Bahama would make them in vogue). Like his dad, Chris found poetry in the music. Each song provided a few minutes of respite from the daily grind.

In 2007, Chris and I headed to the Bama Breeze tour concert south of the city. We settled into to our second-row aisle seats and took in the sounds, smells and energy of the open-air concert. As Jimmy started warming up for "Son of a Son of a Sailor "he must have caught sight of my beautiful tanned, blond haired 13-year-old boy clad in a silk shirt jamming in the aisle. He pointed to Chris and dedicated the song to him. After the song he had a roadie bring a Bama Breeze tour pick to him. When we got home we glued the pick and the ticket to an autographed picture of Jimmy. And Chris kept it all these years as a prized possession.

This January my boy, along with three friends, drowned in a canoe accident in a small lake in Wisconsin. He was 21-years-old. Although the grief at times feels unbearable, there are 21 years of memories of joy that provide some comfort. One of those moments was the Buffett concert on July 21, 2007. Thanks. Jimmy!

I hope you now understand that truly one of my favorite activities is driving in my Jeep, with my boy's spirit at my side listening to Jimmy Buffett and smoking a cigar.

In September of 2016 I scheduled another session with Andrew. Having experienced such a powerful first reading I wasn't sure what I was supposed to do. I wanted desperately to contact him, but he had answered so many questions in June that I wasn't sure what was next. I guess I was fearful that we were done. This was going to be a follow up visit to catch up. I wrote a list of questions for Chris and here is how it went.

Dad: Who are you with?

Chris: Your parents and Jerry

Dad: Tell me something only I know.

I was referring to what we would say when he was a kid. "Well buddy, I guess it's just you and me." "Yep" Chris would say "just the way I like it." Looking at my notes I don't see that he confirmed that.

Dad: did something happen in August with your status?

Chris: No response

Dad: Do you see us daily?

Chris: All the time. Lots of time with my mom.

Dad: Have you made an appearance that I missed?

Chris: I'm with you constantly.

Dad: How do I know it's you?

Chris: Smell and lights

Dad: Does the dog know you are around?

Chris: She looks toward the chair. (There is a blue leather chair in the family room. When Chris would crash on the couch our lab would curl up on the chair next to him)

Dad: What did you think of the golf outing (held in his honor on Sept 10, 2016)? We held the second one on Sept 11, 2017.)

Chris: Andrew reported that he acknowledged the toast with his friends

Dad: Where were you during outing?

Chris: All around, mostly with my friends (some things don't change)

Dad: Do you know when I'm at your grave?

Chris: I go with you.

So, another first for me. A Q & A with my son who crossed over. It was great. It was affirming, but it was also a little bit of a letdown. The first in-person reading in June was so emotionally overwhelming and so charged with spirit energy that I feared a letdown if It doesn't get repeated. It does however get replaced with the knowledge that it's real. There is another world just a rice paper wall away. It's real and my precious son is there. I want to know more. I want to know the rules, and I want in.

Sally knew a wonderful woman from her reading group. The woman, Jenniffer Weigel, was involved with mediums and had herself written some terrific books on the subject. She was hosting events featuring well known mediums at the Wilmette Theatre. A sort of evening of spirit featuring.... you get it. One such event was featuring Thomas John, a sort of medium to the stars type from New York. Sally asked if I wanted to tag along and I enthusiastically agreed. On Tuesday night, December 13, 2016 we met at the theatre. We purposely arrived early so we could get seats near the front. These two things were foreign to me, showing up early and sitting up front. This really had to be important to me, and it was.

The evening started off with Jen and Thomas sitting on the stage discussing his gifts. This was interesting but all I really cared about was my son. There were probably about 100 people in the audience, all hoping for a chance to have this famous medium grace them with a chance to speak with someone they lost. I didn't want to mention this to Sally ahead of time but there was little (I didn't say no) doubt in my mind that Chris would come through. I sat there with a very quiet confidence in my boy. He was tenacious, and unless every medium up to this point was full of it, he was a strong spirit. The first two groups Thomas approached were fascinating. One spirit was a firefighter who had been killed in a collision involving the firetruck. Thomas told his grieving sister that he was not sitting in his usual seat on the firetruck, or his death would have been avoided. The amazed sister confirmed this. He sent messages of love that he was still involved in all of their lives just from a different vantage point. This was getting good. Thomas walked across the theatre to our side. He asked, "Who over here lost their son to drowning? He was in a small boat in cold water with other boys who also crossed." Sally and I stood, and I was handed a microphone. Thomas stated this is not the first time Chris talked to us, and that we had been to other mediums (I hoped Thomas didn't get offended and boot us). He said to Sally that she had seen Rebecca

Rosen and that she was the real deal. Chris said he didn't come through very well that day as it was a weird day. Thomas said, "Wow he is very good looking. "He looks like Brad Pitt." Sally and I smiled and shared the fact that Chris' pals confessed Chris used to tell girls that he was Brad's second cousin and had been an extra in a film or two. When Thomas connected with Chris he squinted his eyes and looked over our shoulder. "Uh huh, yes, yes. "He was talking to Chris, or more accurately he was listening to Chris. Thomas waived his hand over his face as if clearing the air. "Did he smoke a lot of pot?" asked Thomas."

Yeah, he did, responded his mom, to the kind laughter from other parents in the audience. Thomas said that we knew that Chris was never destined to be with us for a long time. He also told us that Chris had a few other near-death experiences not that long before.

Thomas said he came through with the three other boys and they all are fine. Chris told him there were lots of activities prior to this gathering.

Chris told Thomas that he left on this trip to the lake house in Wisconsin from home. Although he was living at a frat house in DeKalb, he was home for Christmas and he indicated that our house was home. And, "Dad no blame." I wasn't sure if he meant I wasn't to blame the people who owned the lake house, the other kids, or myself.

Thomas said that not all the answers came through right away. I don't know what that means but I didn't want to interrupt this reading. Thomas said that Chris hangs around the living room and messes with the TV. He mentioned his funeral that was attended by lots of people and that he loved all the celebration and focus. Thomas said Chris told him to tell us "Claire." Thomas just assumed it made sense to us and it did. He was referring to the Claire who Nancine said Chris was in love with.

Claire's mom Charlotte told Sally that when Chris would visit, he would often remove a sword that was hanging on the wall and play with it. (of course, he did). Claire said one day, after he had crossed, she felt Chris and for no reason the sword fell off the wall. The mount was in place, it had been secure, but it still fell. Charlotte was secure in her knowledge that Chris was letting them know he was still around. Thomas told us that Chris is taking a leadership role on the other side and is working with young people. This was not surprising to Sally and me but still very comforting.

Then, Sally's father Warren popped in. Thomas said that Warren was a big hunter. Thomas indicated that he was a collector and referred to Massachusetts. He referenced a woman named Terry, foreign coins, vases, artifacts. Thomas said that Warren was helping Chris come through.

Warren was absolutely at his best in the field upland bird hunting. It was where he most connected with his sons, and where I enjoyed him the most.

Warren attended Harvard Business School and Sally was born at Mass General Hospital. Terry was Warren's current wife when he passed. Thomas also told us that Warren said he still watches out for Sally's mom, Mary.

Warren was indeed a collector. Ancient pottery, rare coins, art, guns and artifacts, etc. In one of his ventures he actually located and raised a Spanish galleon off the Florida coast, laden with jewels and coins. So.... check, check, check and check.

Sally's father Warren has come through in almost every reading involving her before and after this. That's her story but I will tell you that the gist of it was he was sorry he wasn't a better father to her. I know it gave her some solace although she had already worked through it and made her peace. It was difficult especially in later readings together for me not to tap my feet and look at my watch to indicate we were on the clock because Warren never knew how to tell a short story.

In closing Chris told us that he is with his big white dog on the other side. He also wants us to know he sends us feathers to let us know he's around. (Remember this for later on.) He referred to the blue jacket that Sally now wears (that's one powerful jacket) and he tells Thomas that he is still growing and evolving. Thomas said he is working on his skills in coming through and that he is very funny.

This was absolutely amazing. This was a psychic drive-by of an atomic nature. (too much...maybe) We were just one couple in the audience of a hundred plus hoping against hope to get a brief connection. Instead we got an intimate reading in 10 minutes. It literally was like time stood still while Thomas was connecting with Chris.

CHAPTER SIX:

THE RANCH AND THE BEACH

Now I have to go back a month to November 2016. There were two incidents that only made sense now in hindsight. The first involves a fundraiser for a scholarship to In Balance Ranch Academy, a therapeutic boarding school for teen boys with substance issues. Chris attended the school and stayed on as staff in the role of Life Coach. The school was near and dear to our whole family because we felt it gave us our boy back. As emotional as we knew it would be, nothing could prepare Sally and I for the emotional tsunami that was about to roll over us. Even something as uneventful as walking past the baggage carousel in the Tucson Airport almost made me buckle with despair. I couldn't help but think about the many times I was impatiently waiting for my bags to appear allowing me to walk the 50 yards to the car rental desk ready to start the familiar route to see Chris. I began to weep, almost uncontrollably in the airport. I needed to find my sun glasses and take a deep breath. Unfortunately for Sally, in these instances the despair was always contagious. This hasn't changed in the nearly two years since his crossing. We checked into a resort hotel that Sally and Chris would stay in when she would visit him. We loved to take individual trips to Arizona, so we would each have one-on-one time with our baby boy. Once again, the familiarity of the resort was crushing. Note to self: find a new hotel that didn't hold ghosts of the past wandering the halls, snack bar and pool. We are again attending the fundraiser this year but are staying in a different hotel. See, old dog-new trick.

The fundraiser went well, and we loved being with the Barrasso family that owns the school; they loved our boy like he was one of their own. The guest speaker was warm, funny and very charming. At least I was told I was. The entertainment was provided by Sam Dupont, a professional singer-songwriter, an ex-Ranch kid who was like a brother to my boy. He sang a song called "Stay Put" that he wrote for Chris. They spoke about Chris and showed a tear jerker of a video of his time at The Ranch. The best part for me was the sweet, wonderful, rambunctious teenage boys. I loved them all and saw my Chris in them. The night was wonderful. It was the inaugural fundraiser and it will forever be associated with my lovely boy who was passing into legend status before our eyes.

The next day we met Patrick and Betsy Barrasso for breakfast. Sally, Patrick and I drove south for about 90 minutes to the Ranch. Originally a dude ranch which went under, Patrick bought the property, the buildings and started working on making his dream come true. The Ranch had a school, a handful of bunkhouses for students, mess hall, gym stables and corals, etc. The students learned to take care of the horses. I must admit that I was a bit skeptical of the whole therapeutic equestrian philosophy, but when I began witnessing the progress in my son and his classmates, I became a convert. We arrived at the ranch, had a lovely lunch and went on a tour with Robert, who was a staff supervisor all during Chris' stay. We cherished each step on every path between buildings that we had walked before with Chris. The first day we dropped him off flashed before our tearful eyes. It was bittersweet. He was safe and happy here and I believe a part of him will always be at the Ranch. We were on the deck of the music building looking out at the boys going through their daily paces with their horses. We spoke of Chris' time there with Robert. Robert, a full-blooded Apache, did a hitch in the Air Force, got a college degree and escaped the misery of the reservation. He spoke of Chris and Sam Dupont and remembered giving Sam a feather, that Sam, to this day, carries with him in his guitar case. Robert explained that birds, specifically hawks, can be signs from the dead. He told us to look out for feathers as a sign from Chris. We finished our tour and met back up with Patrick. He and Betsy had an appointment later in Tucson and I guess we were pushing it. We were in his car and halfway down the rutted dirt road (the one Chris flipped his pickup truck on a mere year and a half before). One of his NDE's but that's another story completely. Whenever we were leaving the ranch to go home, Chris and I would embrace at the rental car parked on the half-moon parking lot. That's always where we said our goodbyes. But Patrick had parked in his spot by the office and we were a mile down the dirt road before it hit me. I didn't want to ask Patrick to turn around, but I felt I was somehow letting Chris down. When we made it back to the hotel in the hills around Tucson we didn't say a word. It simply hurt too badly to talk. I tossed and turned all night, and, in the morning, I decided I needed to go back to the ranch. I texted Patrick for the gate code and he suggested I go out around 4 p.m. and he would arrange for me to speak at a group meeting and then have dinner with the boys. Something started settling in my soul and I knew I would be with Chris for sundown. After a round of golf (hey I had to kill time somehow) with my pal Steve at Tucson Country Club, I was on my way to the Ranch with a cigar in hand and Jimmy Buffet on the stereo

It couldn't have gone better. I got there early enough to walk every step of the ranch and talk to Chris as I strolled. The meeting was terrific, and I connected with the boys and they connected with me. We had a meal, some conversation and a lot of love. When it was time to go, I thanked my new pals and some old ones and headed for the half-moon parking lot where my SUV was parked. Here was my moment. I looked up at the desert sky, the stars, the moon and knew I was standing with my boy. I hugged him, left arm over right and told him goodbye. I told him I love him and told him to be good. It was perfect. I could go home now…well almost.

The next morning, we woke up and drove into Tucson to meet with Thad, who had been Chris' therapist at the ranch. We loved Thad and trusted him. Although he no longer worked at the ranch I believe his heart will always be there. We talked of Chris, boys, addiction and recovery. We spoke of love and redemption. We said our goodbyes to Thad. We had one more stop before we flew home. Sally had been in touch with Chris' friend, Steven Gonzales. His little boy Johnny was Christopher's godson, and she had arranged for us to meet in a park near the zoo. The minute we saw this beautiful child something moved in us both. Johnny ran and embraced us. Although his hair was brown and his skin was olive he was so much like our Chris. He was darting back and forth, curious and sweet. We felt our Chris around us all. While walking toward the pond, I saw Sally reach down and pick up a feather. Not long after I did the same. I asked Sally to put mine in her purse and give it to me when we got home. The time with Johnny was magical and so healing. We did what Chris wanted. We connected with his godson and promised to be a part of his life. The day after we returned I went to the grave to catch up with Chris. On his grave along with stones, coins, etc., was the feather I brought from Tucson. "Dammit Sally," I didn't say to leave it on the grave, I wanted it for my office. When I returned home I mentioned that to my bride. "What are you talking about, your feather is where you asked me to leave it…and next time bring your own damn feather home."

This is the God's honest truth. No embellishing, no poetic license. This happened.

The next weekend I was in Sarasota for the wedding of Allen, one of my oldest and closest friends. We have been friends since the first day of high school, at Bishop Timon in South Buffalo, in 1971. We played football together, transferred schools together, chased girls together and drank beer together. All of which he did better than me. We stayed friends through my alcoholism and recovery and the loss of his wife Debbie to cancer a dozen years before. After the weekend in Tucson there are probably two or three people in the world I would get back on a plane for (especially without golf clubs), but Allen was one of them. Allen was getting married and I needed to be there. The wedding was lovely with the reception at a local restaurant/winery. It was so nice to see members of his family, some of whom I've known

for 45 years. I found myself sitting outside enjoying a cigar and the company of a few of his Sarasota pals. I have always had a habit of disappearing at some point in every evening and tonight was no different. It's called the Irish goodbye. After opening the door of an Uber for someone's wife, I saw my opening. I continued across the parking lot and jumped in my rental car. I rolled down the window and lit up a fresh cigar. (I always keep a small aerosol can of air freshener in my shaving kit when I travel for just such occasions.) I looked at my GPS got my bearings and headed for a beach. I didn't know which beach and at the time I probably didn't think it mattered. But it did matter. Although it was a beautiful night, the beach was deserted which may have not been that unusual at 11 p.m. on a Friday night. I parked my car, took off my shoes, rolled up my pants and headed toward the sand. The moon was full and cast a beautiful trail on the water. I began to walk up the beach, cigar in hand, talking to Chris. I felt a chill on the back of my neck and knew he was with me, closer than I have felt him since he crossed. I had no idea why this moment brought our spirits and our energy so close, but it did. He was right there and I knew it. I didn't think it or surmise it - I flat out knew it. I walked and we talked and we reveled in our closeness as we had before he had to go. The moment brings an energy washing over me even as I write this. I see the moon and feel the sand. The following night I again slipped away and went to another beach and he was there again. It was only when Allen came to Chicago for my second annual Chris McQ golf outing did it make sense to me. He mentioned that Siesta Key was considered sacred by the Indians. He told me the sand is actually quartz crystal based. I needed to look into this... and here's what I found in the *Legend of Siesta Key*

The belief in Siesta Beach's concentration of energy has at least some scientific roots that can be documented, and it has to do with Siesta's sand. Whiter than the sand at any other beach in the area, Siesta's sand is also known for its relative coolness even on the hottest of days. Those qualities are derived from the content of sand, which is indeed unique from any other beach in the world Siesta sand is 99.9 percent quartz. This makes the sand appear very white. And because of the way the crystals have been worn down, the sand is exceptionally soft. You also won't find much particulate shell matter.

Siesta's sand originated thousands of years ago from the Appalachian area. That fact is significant to energy healers because of their deep belief that quartz is itself a healing material, especially quartz derived from the area near Hot Springs, Ark. Quartz crystal is a natural conductor of energy. Many healers frequently choose Siesta Beach as the site for meditation events because of the energy they feel is concentrated there. Quartz is one of the highest vibratory minerals of the earth.

I didn't know why that beach was so full of energy. I just knew I felt amazingly close to Chris. The following summer in a private reading with Thomas John, he told me Chris walked right through me that night on the beach. I will go into that reading in more detail later. (I would have said *in due course*, but I just couldn't seem to pull it off.)

CHAPTER SEVEN:

THE FIRST ANNIVERSARY & CHANNEL WRITING

It has now been a year since Chris crossed over. The pain that we have felt individually and shared as a family is almost incomprehensible. The void his crossing has caused in us all will never be filled or healed. There's no way to sugar coat this reality. But I am also very proud that I have been trying to find a connection and some answers in the world of spirit. I don't view this effort as a way to temporarily ease the pain, but rather as a connection that is not bound by accepted philosophy. If there is something there and he is part of it, and if I can connect to it and through it him, I need to find out. And if it all turns to out to be new age nonsense, then I want to move on and try to find another outlet for my grief.

In the past year I have reached out and spoken to three established mediums, all of whom connected with Chris. That number will increase in 2017. I have started meditating and attending spirit groups to try to open my psychic abilities. I wanted to hone my skills. My intention is to sharpen my skills so that I can get closer to my Chris. I want to feel what I felt in Sarasota, all the time. I want to feel the energy and excitement the medium experiences as they send messages from Chris all the time. And unless I want to become a cosmic groupie, or psychic

Dead Head, then I better figure this out. So slowly and unsurely that was what I began to do.

And on the morning of January 3, 2017, one year after Chris' crossing, something clicked. I was awakened at 3 a.m., something that wasn't that unusual. I went into my office, which used to be Chris' bedroom. In the past year I began this practice of sitting at my desk, lighting candles and sage (which to me has the sweet smell of a sweaty athletic teen, so familiar to me) and listening to meditation music. I have pictures of Chris as a young man and a child that I would focus on. My hope was that this meditation would bring him closer to me.

However, this was the anniversary of his crossing. I assumed that the 3 a.m. spirit wakeup call was because this was the time of his crossing. It was only later in conversation with Andrew did I find out that spirits are most active between 3 a.m. and 4 a.m. What happened next was a surprise to me.

On my desk along with some stones purchased around Christmas from *one of those stores,* were pens and a legal pad. During my meditation I picked up the pen and began to write. What follows is the exact conversation with Chris from the other side. I didn't think …. I just began to write.

The first message given was that I should have a cross in my office. This voice (came more like thoughts than a voice) in my head and I am absolutely convinced that was my Christopher crossing back over to reach me.

"It's like a beach, beautiful and pink, warm but the colors are soft and vibrant. Pink, blues and strong green. The air is warm surrounding us. It's air and love (love air) everywhere. Nothing hurts. Warm and happy —always young. Miss you Dad, but I'll see you soon enough. Be nicer to Mom. Try to understand, she feels alone. You don't, you know I'm here and you feel

me...she's not sure. (This will change significantly in the upcoming year.)

No recall or bad memories about drowning. It's all warm and good. Just love. Remember the beach, the colors and soft warm breeze (but not a breeze). Don't be afraid of anything, not health, money, the kids, mom. I'm here, I'm on it. I'm sorry you hurt so bad. But no other way to get out gracefully. You get it, you know, you've been there. I love my friends (I told you they were great loving people) They sure came through huh Pop. So, did you.

I'm with you when you golf, that was one thing that was coming together there. No mistakes Pop. Jerry says hi. Say hello to Uncle Mike (Holmberg) for me (he needs it). I'll help Marcia; she'll be okay, so will you. This is cool, run with it, don't doubt. Use Andrews's pen. Flows like a stream and life. Let's do this again. Mom is sweet. Went to her for love and you for direction. Both love. Read this later. Feels like a dream huh pop. It's me. Smiling at you Pop. Hugging you-so close. Forget the date- all the dates. I'm waiting for you Pop. Why are you even questioning? Andrew, Nancine, and Thomas. I talked to you! On the beach in Sarasota, it was me. You knew it then. You were my world Pop. You're embarrassed to write it but it was true. We'll be together, just like Scottsdale, just you and me.

Don't be mad at Scottie. He's just him. Feel me Pop, around the back of your head and neck- It's me. I'm crying too. Just glad to be with you. Think about warm every day, like Hawaii. Doing good Pop. Like an angel (like) that's me. Pop, Nancine was for real. Andrew sees me and the other guys too. I'm here! Mom's gal saw me, I'm here. The girl on my birthday, well not so much, but she tried.

It's natural writing not printing. I wasn't good at cursive! Remember- play place. Fine motor skills no problem now. Stay with me Pop, I'm still here. I was cold, but I wasn't lonely, I was with my friends. We have good friends Pop! I still do and do here."

> I noticed the time....*3:49 a.m. Chris* wrapped it up. *"I had already crossed fully. Go to bed Pop. I love you. Talk soon."*

Whoa...this was going to take some processing. I turned on the desk lamp and I reread the messages. Was this just my way of dealing with the grief? Was I just trying to make myself feel better and more important to my son who crossed. I didn't think so. I was also pretty sure I wasn't doing this for attention. I have subsequently shown these writings to Andrew Anderson, Sheri Jewel and Thomas John, all respected mediums, and they all confirmed they are from Chris. I guess that's as close to a stamp of approval as you can get in the psychic world.

Let's look at the message. Chris loved the beach and we shared a love for anything tropical (including umbrella drinks, him not me). We both felt happy in that setting. Chris referred to not having bad memories about the drowning which is the same message that we gratefully heard from mediums. The thought of his last moments has haunted his mother and me. There were a number of things in the message that sounded like me and of course gave me pause. I have also subsequently looked up what was happening, and it had a name. Channel writing. I thought it was automatic writing. However, one of the aspects of automatic writing is that the handwriting is dissimilar. But this was done in my own handwriting., cursive, not printed. (which is a little strange as I usually print because my writing is almost illegible.) This writing is somewhat clear for me. I thought as I wrote this book that what I was experiencing was automatic writing. But as my knowledge of the subject grew I discovered it was really channel or spirit writing. Chris also referred to his own fine motor skills issues, and *the play place.* This referred to a therapy class for his fine motor skills. Chris had problems with fine motor skills. Although he could throw and catch a baseball, the finer skills such as handwriting were a challenge. I was only there once with him and hadn't thought of it in 16 years. Now it's starting to come into focus. He also referred to his friends being great loving people and how they came through. They all did, particularly his NIU classmates who came enmasse to the wake and funeral. They would meet me at his grave and stop by the house for a visit. And he said this, twelve hours before they all showed at his grave for an impromptu celebration of his life on the anniversary of his crossing. He is right; they are great people. One other message that proved accurate was that he told me not to be *mad at Scottie, because he was just being himself.* This was not a thought that would originate from me. Chris had two distinct group of friends. There were the kids whom he grew up with on the north shore and then, his frat brothers from Northern, whose backgrounds were more diverse. We love them all but have a strong bond and a shared loyalty with those NIU kids. I know they loved and were loved by my boy. In the first year after Chris' crossing we would attend the Penguin Players Production as we became donors to their cause. They have actually set up a Chris McQuillen Spirit Award & Scholarship for a student mentor in Chris' honor. On those occasions and at other times, we would stop by the frat house with a couple of cases of Stella on ice and a box of cigars. The boys would all come together and spend an evening with *Chris' family.* One night, not long after his passing they held a Rose Ceremony honoring Chris and presenting Sally with a rose. They presented me with a framed Bills Jersey in his favorite number signed by every member of AKL. As I write this book I can see it above my computer screen mounted on my wall. The room where the ceremony was held became the Chris McQ room, with photos and jerseys adorning the walls. (along with Chris' Buffalo Bills Flag). They moved the pool table up from the basement to this room which was very appropriate since he spent more time playing pool than attending any class. The pool table now has blue and red Buffalo Bills pool balls. After one of these sessions Sally said it was too bad we didn't have this kind of relationship with these boys while Chris was still on this side. My response was simply that until Chris crossed we were just another pair of parents. Some of Chris' local pals make it a habit to stop by the house on Thanksgiving, when they're home from college to crack a cold one and reminisce. God, we love these two groups of kids.

Most of Chris' AKL pals have moved out of frat house or graduated. We stay close to them but our connection to the frat house itself has faded. In the first year it was a gift to go there and feel him, but the boys moving on from the house gave us closure. Chris' AKL pals and gals organized a 100-person pub crawl to celebrate his 23rdbirthday on April 15, 2017. I drove to Naperville, where it was being held, to buy a bunch of pitchers, hug and kiss the kids and then swing by his grave to release a Chinese lantern with Sally.

But of course, I have gotten off track. So, when Chris told me to "be nice to Scottie," I know it didn't originate with me. Scottie was the young man whose parents owned the lake house where the boys drowned. When I drove up to recover my son on January 3, I was surprised to find the parents weren't there. But Chris loved Scottie and Scottie loved Chris. And Chris felt it important that I be prepared to be kind to Scottie and put any resentment aside. Okay, Chris, only for you. Besides when will I ever need to show him kindness? Well flash forward to twelve hours later at his grave. Along with 22 of his friends, Scottie approached me with tears in his eyes. He was there to visit his beloved friend Chris, and I was able to embrace him and, in my heart, forgive him. Chris was right of course. It wasn't his fault. Scottie didn't need forgiving. There was no malice in his broken heart.

When Chris referred to getting out gracefully it struck a chord. It was only after he crossed that his mom and I admitted that we always feared we would only have him for a short time. He had a number of close calls and one, possibly two near death experiences (NDE). I really wished I would have delved more deeply into those with him, but I just assumed it was him going into shock. He did mention a Man in the mine shaft with him. We can now conclude it was his guardian angel. Chris had some issues with depression and we were always worried about that when he drank. I have experienced suicide in my family growing up and it was anything but graceful. It was messy and awkward and painful. Again, I'm not interpreting what he said. I'm just reporting it. You figure it out for yourself. However, I don't believe we are predestined. I don't think we are God's chess pieces. I believe that we have paths to walk that are determined by our free will. We always have choices. I also believe Chris had been given some heavenly hall passes in the past. I don't know the rules or why he ran out of them. I have been told there are exit points in your life where you can choose to cross. I don't know how or if that is true. I guess I will know eventually though.

He referred to Scottsdale. I would pick up Chris in Tucson and we would head to a hotel or a resort in Scottsdale. We first did this for Thanksgiving, 2010. We loved spending time together, waking whenever we wanted, eating what we wanted and watching movies when we wanted. It was heaven for me to look over and see my Chris sleeping in the bed next to me. He was warm, safe and happy. Scottsdale trips would later include spring training baseball games, golf and the addition of his brother Will, his Uncle Mike Sawyer and Chris' beloved girlfriend, Gali. Those days make me smile and keep me going when I'm otherwise stalling out.

He told me to use Andrew's pen, so let me explain. At a group session at his home Andrew handed me a Bic Velocity pen. I was using it with this conversation with Chris. He told me to use that pen so of course I use it for every channel writing and medium session. Hey, Chris wants me to use the pen and I trust him. He also told me, "You were my world, Pop. You're embarrassed to write it, but it was the truth." I can promise you that this didn't originate with me. But as long as we are on the subject, you were and are my world Christopher."

So, let's put this all in the category of, well I guess this isn't bullshit. How else do you explain it? It was actually the point that cemented the reality of it for me. I now knew this was real and it was a way for me to be able to connect with my son.

On January 16, 2017 I woke up at 3 a.m. and walked to my office. I lit the candle, burned the sage, aligned my chakras and listened to meditation music. I was awaiting a connection. What else could my son tell me? My pen began to write on the legal pad… "Not the right time. Go back to work Pop. Thanks for doing the wristbands for my friends. I love you too, Pop."

Was my son blowing me off from another dimension? Well, one thing rings true from mediums about spirits. Their personalities don't change when they cross. I remember a time when I had booked all of us on a spring break to the Florida Keys. Chris' friend Jimmy and his dad were going to Mexico, reserving a suite of rooms and traveling on a private jet. They invited Chris to come along. "What do ya think dad? You gotta admit it's a better offer." I couldn't argue with him then, and sure wouldn't now. If he couldn't visit with me I can only assume he had a better offer. I can't help loving that kid. I had wrist bands made for his first golf outing that had "Life is honestly so beautiful…." printed on them, a reference to his saying "Life is honestly so beautiful as long as you allow it to be." These bands weren't great quality and the words were not embossed. And they began to rub off. I had them redone and sent to his pals. It was sweet of Chris to thank me. He sure does love his friends.

On Jan 18, 2017 I walked in my office later than usual and began to rush through my ritual.

I picked up my pen and began to write...

"This is the time of day for me. Don't schedule so close Pop. We need more time. You always cut it too close. You don't need your glasses, it's not you writing. I loved it when you picked me up. Faith...Believe... I'm here. Remember fishing in Florida. You did that for us...for me. (interestingly enough, the fishing comes up in a future impromptu reading with a medium in November of 2017.) *Don't try so hard; it's not a trance. It's just a chat. Missing you too, Pop. No matter what they say. This is our time Pop. Now you know. Get up early for this Pop. Ask Andrew about this. Go to your appointment, Pop. – See you*

One thing that stood out with this conversation was that he said he missed me too. *"No matter what they say."* I felt this was in response to a question I asked a medium early on after Chris' crossing. I was told the spirits don't miss us as we miss them because they are right here all around us. I was also told it's tough to miss the ones on our side because what they have is so amazing. However, I do believe they miss the contact with us, especially the physical closeness and the hugs for example. I feel Chris misses those as much as I do.

Now, let's recap. My son who has been pretty strong in coming through with mediums has found a way to slow his energy down enough to contact his cosmic slug of a dad. And although just getting his message on the anniversary of his crossing would have been an amazing gift, it looks as if this could turn into a continuing dialog. What I need to do is enhance this interaction. What can I do to facilitate his contact with me? I actually picked up a book called, *Complete Idiot's Guide to Communicating with Spirits*. I kid you not! Repetition helps, but as with golf, repeating a bad swing only "helps get you worse." I am more than willing to read, listen, and attend lectures with those who do this well and often. In this case I am greedy, and I want more.

On January 22, at 3:45 a.m. Chris came through again. I started going through my pre-game routine (throwback to my locker room days). I had a picture of Chris and me in Iowa after my niece Jamie's wedding in October 2014. We were standing together at a street fair, shoulders touching, smiling and enjoying the moment. When I began to meditate that morning, I folded the picture in half, so I could concentrate on Chris' image. He was paying attention.

"Keep the picture together pop. Wanted to see if you would get up for this. Thanks pop. Warm and soft, I'm good pop. Miss you. You can feel me around your neck. That's me. Like when the angels were around you before. It comes from over here to you."

"It wasn't a good fit on your side. It is now over here. Been thinking of me when I was little, sure did love you pop. This is me, Andrew will tell you. Thanks for setting this up, it means the world to me. You're the one pop, always were. Trusted you and knew you were there. Left side is creative side. (don't over think this) Just talking. All the time in the world. You can keep the notes in your head and your heart if you miss some. Candle... low glow means I'm here. Taking off pop. Cheers. Dumb meditation music sounds like a phone."

After a session I check to see if my writing is legible and then I go to bed. It usually takes more time than you would think. The next day I reviewed the reading and looked online about the left side creative reference from Chris. I thought he was wrong but according to Google:

> *The left side of the brain is responsible for controlling the right side of the body. It also performs tasks that have to do with logic, such as in science and mathematics. On the other hand, the right hemisphere coordinates the left side of the body and performs tasks that have do with creativity and the arts.*

Chris told me not to overthink it. Of course, I did and of course he was right, again. I loved the fact that he wanted me to unfold the picture, to concentrate on us together. We were always terrific together and it felt good for him to acknowledge that. I always finish with a sense of awareness, a strong sense of his being, followed the next day by flat out missing him terribly.

Let me go into my pregame ritual. It's not as random as it sounds. It starts with dragging my old body out of bed and into my office. I then turn on a desk lamp; lately it's a green banker's lamp that was Christopher's. Remember my office is in the room that was Chris' bedroom so there is an amazing amount of good energy flowing in here. I close my laptop to darken the space. I light a few candles. I then light some sage. I always use a sage stick made of California white sage. The reason I use white California sage is because I like it. (I don't use scented sage for the same reason I don't drink flavored coffee.) I then spread the smoke in the air with the feather I brought from Tucson. I have pulled out a few pictures of Chris and prop them up so as to concentrate on them during meditation. I make sure that my desk is clear of anything on the writing surface besides my velocity pen and the same brand of white legal pad I get from Staples. All these rituals worked, once, then again and I don't want to risk breaking a connection. I then pull out a sheet or more precisely a Chakra chart that Andrew gave me, focusing from bottom to top all seven chakras (the focal points in the body used for meditation). I have headphones on my phone and connect to random meditations to contact the other side. I begin the meditation and try to let go. I'm holding a crystal in my hand and have numerous small stones on the front of my desk that I may pick up during any point of the meditation. Lately I've begun to sprinkle a small amount of sand from Siesta Key on the legal pad. I generally feel Chris around me before I hear him. Once the meditation music is done, I start getting messages from Chris and I write them down. It's always the same way. I write in the dark in cursive. When the session is over, I pull out a fine point pen to make notes of clarification. This is actually quite taxing because I am emotionally drained and physically tired. It's usually well after 4 a.m. by this time. I then shut it down by blowing out candles and turning on lights. I either head back to bed for an hour or so or start the day.

Just a couple of days later, on January 25, we were at it again.

"I'm here pop. I like the song. Needed you to wake up. You can't go in the hole pop. You know better. They need you. See the candle light pop, that's me. In the car writing the song that was me. We're already together pop, you know that. Glad you reached out to Maggie, it made me smile. She made me smile, for a while anyhow. Good to feel close and reconnect. Don't drift off pop. You're my connection… toughen up…I love you."

CHAPTER EIGHT:

I'LL SEND YOU FEATHERS

Chris was referring to a song during the reading. My dear and talented pal Brad and his wife Jane came over for dinner on a Saturday in mid-January. Brad and I have collaborated on some songs together and we ended up in my home office discussing music. I ended up telling him about Robert from Tucson and the story of the feathers. I openly talked about the signs and my contact with Chris on the other side. Brad is one of the kindest guys I have ever met, and he is a brilliant musician. We finished the evening along with a Chicago Style Lou Malnatti's pizza. A couple of days later Brad sent me a recording of the opening verse to a song. ***I'll send you feathers***. I grabbed a pad and pen and began to write the song as I drove home that night. It flowed. Chris was right next to me in the jeep as I wrote, cried and sang his song. When I got home I raced to my computer and after some back and forth with Brad, here is the result. A few weeks later we went to the studio and Brad recorded it. I've included a link for sound cloud where a number of songs for Chris are included. You can find *I'll send you feathers* there. I still cry when I hear it …

I'LL SEND YOU FEATHERS

---

https://soundcloud.com/tributetochrismcquillen

Wipe your tears, I had to go
There is something that I want you to know
I'll be with you, I'll send you a sign, always know I'll be there to remind you
We'll be together in heaven, in that season
The time we will treasure
Until then. I'll send you feathers

My days were long, my nights were warm
You did your best to keep me safe from the storm
I felt your love, there was no doubt
How could you know that the sand would just run out
We'll be together in heaven, in that season
The time we will treasure
Until then … I'll send you feathers.

We had no time, for sweet goodbyes
I see the pain in those soft Irish eyes
I'm trying hard to let you know
I'll be here at the end of your road show
We'll be together in heaven, in that season
The time we will treasure
Until then … I'll send you feathers.

A little side story about Feathers that I asked Brad to tell in his words

"So, shortly after Joe and I finished writing and recording the song, "I'll Send You Feathers," I was driving up to meet Joe for golf and listening to WXRT in Chicago and their Sunday morning program called "Breakfast with the Beatles." Terri Hammert, the DJ, was interviewing Julian Lennon and she asked him, "So Julian please tell me about your White feather Foundation." I perked right up and turned the radio up only to hear Julian explain, "Well shortly before my dad died he told me, should anything happen to me I'm going to send you a feather." To which Terri replied, "Wow that was odd. What did you think of that"?" Julian said, "Well like most things dad said we thought it odd and we carried on. But, about a year and a half or so after his death, I was on tour in Australia and sitting in my hotel room and the manager of the hotel rang and said, 'Excuse me Mr. Lennon, but there is an Aborigine tribe in the lobby of our hotel and they are demanding to see you as they have a gift for you. What would you like me to do?'" Julian went down to the lobby and the chief of the tribe approached him while unwrapping a large white feather that "the great spirit" in the outback of Australia had told him to present this feather to Julian.

I welled up with emotion as the son of my deceased childhood musical hero was communicating his love for his son thru an ancient tribe in Australia. I shared this story with Joe on the golf course on that beautiful summer morning as we hugged and said a prayer.

Are you connecting the dots yet? God, I hope so

Chris also referred to a Maggie. She was a crush from NIU, a recent heart break. I reached out on Facebook just to say hi.

Just last week I met some of his pals at his grave, and there was Maggie. She is a sweet gal and I know why his heart skipped a beat when he saw her.

The kids had a few beers and a few cigars. A couple of days later the December cold killed the dozen peach roses Maggie had left at his grave. Did I mention how much I love those kids?

I sent the song to Andrew but didn't hear anything in response. I wasn't even sure he listened to it. But, hey I heard directly from Chris that he liked the song. How many kinds of affirmation do I need?

A few weeks later, on February 8, 2017, Andrew texted me. He asked me to call him when I had a few uninterrupted minutes to talk. I was finishing up my day, so I waited until I got to my jeep to call him. Something happened today, Andrew said. "Something pretty strange." If a medium is saying that something strange is happening, I knew I'd better put the jeep back in park and listen. Andrew told me that he was running at the gym today when Chris was jogging next to him. Andrew politely asked Chris to come back at another time and Chris declined his polite request. Andrew just didn't know what he was dealing with. Chris was a tenacious kid, a true force of nature in this world or the next. So, Chris continued to run with Andrew and told him he had a poem for me that he wanted to dictate and now was as good as any time to do that. Andrew decided that he probably was out of options, so he acquiesced. Smart man. Andrew was listening to music on his I phone so he called his daughter and asked her to take down a poem from a spirit while he finished his run. I don't know if Andrew will ever decide to write a book, but if he does, this has to be included.

When Chris was finished, Andrew's daughter took an iPhone photo of the poem written on a yellow legal pad. Andrew then forwarded it to me.

I keep a copy in my notes and look at it often.

Thank you pop for the man you've been, you made my life quite full.

The things you've done since I've been gone have touched my heart and soul.

My spirit is always with you pop every step of the way.

Helping you get through the rough, this each and every day.

Even though you cannot see me and there's nothing I can do.

I know you hear my whispers when I say that I love you.

Keep the family strong, and know that I'm still there.

And I'll keep leaving feathers to let you know I care.

So, think about this. I have a message from Robert about feathers. A feather appears almost immediately to Sally and me while we're visiting Chris' godson Johnny in a park in Tucson. Sally brings both feathers back to our home. The next day when I visit Chris at his grave another feather is lying across the stone. Brad is inspired to write a song after hearing the story and Chris says we need to write a song about the signs. Then Chris gets into the act by dictating a poem about feathers to a somewhat reluctant medium.

After this story circulates, I start getting photos emailed by my pals showing feathers in their path or on the golf course. Chris' godfather told me that while focusing on a difficult decision he raised his eyes to the sight of a white feather hovering at eye level in Manhattan. He thanked Chris for the support.

Another symbol mediums told me I would receive from Chris was a red bird, specifically a cardinal. I truly never paid any attention to them. But I have learned that birds and red birds or cardinals were chosen as signs or a messenger from a loved one. Don't ask me why cardinals were selected; I have no clue.

However, I do notice them now. I notice them when I sit in my hot tub gazing through tree branches, thinking about Chris. And I've noticed them in branches hanging over his grave site. Last year while on my annual men's golf trip to Florida, the four of us were on a t- box on the back nine, Michael, Chris' godfather tapped me on the shoulder. He pointed to a branch hanging over the tee box and there sat a big ole cardinal. Looking back and forth at the four faces looking directly at him. "Hi, Chris" was the unsolicited response from each of my three friends. "Hi son, thanks for visiting, "was mine.

My youngest, Christopher's little brother William, had been hitting a wall since Chris' crossing. He was a state ranked high school lacrosse player, and a solid B student. His plan was to play college lacrosse, hopefully on a scholarship. With the loss of his big brother and his fourth concussion things started to unravel. Being 17 is a tough enough age without the world turning upside down with the loss of your older brother. To make matters worse, a couple of months after his brother's crossing, the day of the varsity lacrosse tryout, one of the classes featured a film ending with a teen drowning. Obviously, the tryout didn't go well. The lack of sensitivity by both the education and athletic department is astounding to me to this day. William couldn't talk about the loss. Chris had not been a great older brother. But as of late William's athletic accomplishments, confidence and downright coolness had begun to win Chris over. "Oh man," Chris said to me. "Will is the man. He's so much cooler than I was at his age." That was high praise from the new Will McQ convert.

William knew about his mom and my efforts to reach Chris on the other side. However, I didn't know what he thought of this work. Although his sister Caroline dismissed it all, we had no idea what Will thought. I asked him if he would like to go with me to visit Andrew Anderson, the medium who had become a friend. Although Andrew generally didn't do weekend sessions he agreed to meet with William on Sunday, February 5, 2017.

I gave William a note pad and a pen to keep notes. (He recorded the session instead) but hey I can always use another pad and pen. I was told by both William and Andrew (who was very limited in what he would reveal other than saying that Chris came storming through the session), that the reading was amazing. Will told me Chris referred to both of their struggles with depression. Chris also told him he liked that Will wore the cologne I had gotten Chris for his last Christmas on this side in 2015. I of course didn't know this. Chris made references to certain clothes of his that Will wore, and he told Will he approved of his plan to get the family crest tattooed on his arm just like his. William confided that the only person he told this to was his girlfriend. There was a lot more to the reading that Will keeps in his heart. But the key thing was that Chris came through and told him he loved him. Will's spirit was so very light that day. While driving into Wrigleyville to pick up Buffalo wings, (how else do you improve on a successful medium contact?), Will asked me if he could celebrate the reading with a cigar. I picked out a mild one and we smoked and talked. In my heart I thanked Chris for coming through and bringing some joy to his little brother. He sure deserved it.

On Valentine's day. Or more accurately St. Valentine's day, Chris paid me a 3 a.m. visit.

"Good to talk to William. Made a difference. Mom's doing better, I miss her too. Happy Valentine's Day Momma. You never forgot me- don't today. Put one on my grave. I'll see it…I'll get it. I know your heart is broken. Leave me a heart. It's nicer here than you could imagine- no stress pop- no bullshit. Glad's Will is on board- Caroline will come around. Don't worry. Thanks for getting up. Easy to stay in bed. But I missed you. Don't forget me pop- you are my rock (like the angel told you so long ago). I like the Wrigley story. Put it on Facebook. Glad you are writing those. Keeps you close to me and my young spirit- love the story- keep looking. Don't cry pop I'm here. Meditate before the two mediums- I'll be there. Tell Jimmy happy anniversary from me. Leave him a chip - ☺ from me. I should have followed you, but it's written you know. I'm home. I love you guys. Tell mom again and again. She never forgot Easter or Valentine's day ☺ my momma. She loved me, she loves me. I feel it so strongly. Did you love the poem- inspired by me mostly? How's my dog? She sees me. She doesn't know any better, it's just me. Where do we go from here? Keep working on it pop. Love how hard you are trying. I'm a strong spirit pop, Me!

Will is doing better – this guy will help I know. Good music this time. No phone ☺

Tell Andrew Hi… he knows. Thanks for the poem.

Pretty good right? Gonna head out but you sit there a while. Stay Quiet- Love you so."

Chris--- Your Boy.

PS "You don't need to push this. It's me. Nice right. Enough with the smiley faces. I'm still cool over here. Go look for the Chip!!!"

Well, let's start at the top of the Valentine's Day reading. First and foremost, I am so grateful and touched that Chris would take the time to connect with me on this side. I am so proud of his ability. I love his sensitivity and humor. I really appreciate that he brings things out that I wouldn't say, and in a way, I wouldn't say them. This, along with confirmation from every medium I have contacted, allows me the ability to accept this fabulous gift from my Christopher. When we make the connection, he talks to me.

Chris refers to talking to William. He also told me his momma was doing better. I had to take his word for it. Sally and I had our own path, our own way of grieving. When we shared with each other the grief was overwhelming like a Tsunami. It's difficult to understand unless you've lived it. It makes you broken hearted and lonely. I have been fortunate to have a couple of friends who have also experienced an overwhelming loss. My pal Matt Hayes lost his daughter to cancer when she was a college student. We follow a similar spiritual path and I have prayed with him at his daughter's bed side and felt her spirit. He is on the path, but early in his journey. This book is for guys like Matt. Right before Christmas we were having a burger along with Chris' godfather, Michael. We were discussing holiday plans when I blurted out that Christmas sucks. "It's my second Christmas, almost two full years, and I'm still in pain when I think of the holidays without him."

"Yeah, I know," said Matt. "I know." He meant that I need to get used to it. He was giving a straight answer without any BS. I love that guy.

My other friend who has walked this path is Al Conrad. I've talked about him earlier. He is very much like a brother to me. Thirteen years ago, Allen's wife Debbie succumbed to cancer. I was actually with them both a few days before she passed. Debbie knew our story and knew that Al always looked out for me. I promised her I would do the same for him now. Al found his spirituality through that horrible loss. He was lost and now he's found. Because I knew that he knew I could just drop the rock with Al. He would say, "Can I give you some advice?" and for most people the answer is no. But I paid attention to Al. "During this initial time of grief," Al said, "Hold your tongue. Show restraint. Let's face it neither one of us suffers fools gladly, or at all." Al told me, "I spent the first six months after Debbie's death letting people know how stupid they are, or how lame their statements were. I spent the next year trying to fix the wreckage of those relationships. People don't know, they can't know. But we know, you and me, and that's enough." God put Allen squarely in my path of grief and I grabbed hold. It was comforting when I thought no one knows my pain that he does. My brother Al does.

Below is a wonderful description of the kind of grief I'm referring to. The words below are from a book of blessings called *Benedictus* by the Irish poet and philosopher John O'Donohue who also no longer lives on earth. I hope these words comfort you, as they do me.

When you lose someone you love,
Your life becomes strange,
The ground beneath you becomes fragile,
Your thoughts make your eyes unsure;
And some dead echo drags your voice down
Where words have no confidence
Your heart has grown heavy with loss;
And though this loss has wounded others too,
No one knows what has been taken from you
When the silence of absence deepens.

Flickers of guilt kindle regret
For all that was left unsaid or undone.

There are days when you wake up happy;
Again inside the fullness of life,
Until the moment breaks
And you are thrown back
Onto the black tide of loss.
Days when you have your heart back,
You are able to function well
Until in the middle of work or encounter,
Suddenly with no warning,
You are ambushed by grief.

It becomes hard to trust yourself.
All you can depend on now is that
Sorrow will remain faithful to itself.
More than you, it knows its way
And will find the right time
To pull and pull the rope of grief
Until that coiled hill of tears
Has reduced to its last drop.

Gradually, you will learn acquaintance
With the invisible form of your departed;
And when the work of grief is done,
The wound of loss will heal
And you will have learned
To wean your eyes
From that gap in the air
And be able to enter the hearth
In your soul where your loved one
Has awaited your return
All the time.

That poem touches my soul. When the poet refers to being ambushed by grief, I nod, and find comfort that he knows and others also know.

So back to the St. Valentine's Day message. Chris referred to the fact that his momma never forgets Valentine's Day, Easter, or any holiday. No matter where Chris was he would get a Valentine's box of chocolate from his adoring momma. He wanted to be sure that she didn't forget him. Of course, she didn't; she absolutely couldn't, as she was always so madly in love with her first born. When I went to the grave that day I found a rock in the shape of a heart on his grave. I knew and he knew his mom had been there ahead of me. He also assured me that his world is nicer than I could imagine. That was his gift to me—knowing that he was okay and happy. Chris referred to a message I received from the angels years ago during a period when I had massive stress from my job. I felt like I was melting and I received a message that said "return to the rock." I always assumed it meant to dig deep inside and man up, but it could also mean reach for the source (God). Either way I got through that rough stretch. Back then it was enough to make it through the day and get home to Christopher. He was about six at the time and we would just hang out watching TV until he would fall asleep next to me. I believe he saved my life then, or at least kept me intact.

The amount of information I received from him in a few handwritten pages was amazing. He wanted me to extend his congratulations to Jimmy (Crane) for two years of sobriety. He wanted me to leave a two-year chip on Jimmy's dad's grave, which I of course did. His dad crossed in 2009 and his grave is maybe twenty paces away from Chris'. They always liked each other. It brings me comfort that he is around Chris.

Chris told me, "I should have followed you, but it's written you know. I'm home." I can only assume that he was referring to my years of sobriety. But that wasn't his path. I wished it was. But he does hammer home the message that he's home. Chris tells me how much he loves his momma and acknowledges that he can feel how much she loves him. He referred to the poem he sent Andrew and validated that he inspired it. A few months later this is the exact message I got from Thomas John, the Manhattan Medium.

Good music this time referred to a previous meditation music that sounded like a phone ringing, at least to him. And although the smiley faces came to me on the legal pad, he needed to bust my stones about how many there were. Sorry, Chris. Just trying to follow your script.

Chris referred to the Wrigley story. I had previously written a couple of true stories about Chris. One was about a Jimmy Buffett concert that I included earlier and the other is "Playing at Wrigley "which I will now post

PLAYING AT WRIGLEY!

In 2004 I received an invite to participate in a pickup baseball game at Wrigley Field by Chevrolet. Each dealer could have one participant in the game and one guest to watch from the stands. This was the very first time an outing like this was to take place in the friendly confines.

Having played a lot of ball growing up I dug up my glove and spikes and had my ten-year-old grab his glove which was a lot less dusty than mine. Although he was only supposed to be watching from the stands, it's always good to be prepared in case the fates smile on you and gives you a shot.

As we walked into the gates we were greeted by our Chevy hosts who gave us both a jersey and showed us the way to the dugout (for me) and stands (for Chris). As I headed to the dugout, I grabbed my boy and indicated he should follow me to the dugout. Sitting in the dugout we were approached by a young woman carrying a clip board (a sure sign of authority). As she scanned the list for both of our names she couldn't find Chris' (of course she couldn't... it wasn't there). I suggested she check again. As she scanned the clipboard Chris' big green eyes got very big. "That's okay son," I said. "The nice young lady will find it." "Well, "she said looking at my beautiful hopeful boy, "we'll just write it in. Do you bat righty or lefty? And for the announcement and scoreboard should it be Chris or Christopher?" The baseball gods did smile on us that day and we were in. There was no one in the world with whom I would have rather shared this experience.

We took the field and it was magic. Mickey Morandini coached our team and Milt Papas coached the other. Here we were on the infield of Wrigley!!!HOLY COW!!!When it was our turn to bat, I heard Chris' name announced over the PA system and saw his name in lights. He made solid contact and flew out. When I was up I nervously faced the pitching machine and tried to stare it down. (Tip to self: you can't intimidate metal.) I took a fast ball (really medium speed but it's my story) toward center. Knowing there was no way this old man could go yard at a MLB park I was willing to settle for warning track. (I rounded first as my hit settled in short right center field (very shallow right center field). But hey I was on!

As the innings rolled by we were in the bottom half of a five-inning game, Chris came to the plate. He singled between short and center and I thought my heart would burst. For the moment, all of his 10-year-old self-doubt and insecurities were replaced with a huge smile and a bunny hop on first base. The world was perfect for that moment. A single and a botched throw brought Chris to third base with the game tied.

Mickey Morandini was coaching third and was resting his left arm on my boy's helmet. (a photo op if I ever saw one). A crack of the bat and Mickey sent Chris sprinting for home. The ground ball made its way to the third basemen's glove, and he was preparing for a game saving throw to the plate. Chris beat the throw with a slide and he won the game. What he didn't know was that the third base coach protected his decision to send his favorite base runner by grabbing the third baseman's arm while winking at him. The game was over and the team rushed the plate hugging and high fiving my very proud and elated son. I knew that moment would be one that I would carry in my heart all the rest of my days. Not a bad day for a kid who was supposed to watch from the stands.

Although at the time we were Sox fans (Chris' first Sox game was when he was a month old…staying for fireworks night was a bad idea btw). Chris and I attended many Sox games, including the Al Star game in 2003, as well as when A.J. Pierzynski dropped third strike against the Angels in the AL championship game, and most notably game 2 of the 2005 World Series, with the Paul Konerko's grand slam and the Scotty Pod's homer in the ninth.

While attending NIU, Chris struck a deal with his friend and roommate Raul Esparza, and the rest of the AKL fraternity that if they became Buffalo Bills fans (Buffalo being my hometown and Chris' hometown in his heart), he would become a Cubs fan. His little brother William followed suit. The Bills flag still hangs in the AKL chapter room honoring Chris

On November 2, when the Cubs won the World Series, I know Chris was with Raul and his pals popping cold ones, hugging each other and unabashedly crying.

I often feel my boy around me during times of celebration, I didn't feel him that night, but that was all right. I knew just where his spirit was that night and how happy they all were!

My thanks to Garret Dvorsy, Adrian Faruch (I know), and my buddy Billy Mahon for giving my boy many baseball memories and a baseball legacy he carries with him in heaven.

CHAPTER NINE:
_____

In Person... Again

On February 23, we went to see Rebecca Rosen at the Chicago Sheraton. We decided to take Sally's nephew, Charlie, with us, because he was close with Chris and it was his birthday. It was a packed house and of course we were hoping to connect with our boy. Looking around at the crowd, I thought that I should have paid for VIP seats, wondering if sitting closer to the stage gets us a better shot at connecting. Sally was already a Rebecca Rosen believer after seeing her in Colorado, and I had just finished one of her books. Rebecca started the event by discussing her life and her gift and then jumped right in. The crowd immediately began to annoy me. When Rebecca would move to an area and ask, "Is there anyone named Mary Ann on the other side?" Someone would jump up and say, "I have a grandfather named Marty who passed." Rebecca was very patient as she explained that a female spirit named Mary Ann is not the same as a grandfather named Marty. I wanted to yell out, "Sit down stupid, it's not even close" but I didn't want to get thrown out before giving Chris a chance to make contact.

In a few minutes Rebecca started moving in our direction. I'm telling you we were squarely in the center row smack dab in the middle of the crowd. To be honest with you I absolutely expected Chris to come through as he has in every situation, before or after. I wasn't disappointed. To be perfectly honest, I was so proud I was beaming. Rebecca walked over and announced, "A young man who drowned in cold water is here. He was 21 or 22…" I raised my hand and Rebecca approached us.

"He loves the tattoo," she also said he was referring to a tattoo with wings on it. She asked us, "Who has the connection with him with country music?" Sally and I both claimed that connection. I had exposed Chris to many of my favorite singer songwriters and groups, mostly from the 70s, including Jimmy Buffett, CSNY, Gordon Lightfoot and Bat McGrath. Chris reciprocated by exposing me to the new country singers like Brad Paisley, Eric Church, the Zak Brown Band, etc. I really loved it, especially since it was endorsed by my Chris. Rebecca said she heard one song as clear as day in her head. It was Tim McGraw's "*Live Like You Were Dying.*" If you don't know it, put down this book, google it, listen, and take in every word. This song is special to me as it is a song that we perform, as a band, that was put together, first to entertain the boys at In Balance Ranch when Chris was a Life Coach there, and later at the annual golf outing in Chris' honor. We named the band Frat Dog after Chris' fraternity 's mascot, Cooper. (The dog and his name actually come up in a later reading.) It is the song that unites our souls when we are performing it. Rebecca mentioned the tattoo. In typical McQuillen fashion our 17--year-old William, went with his cousin Charlie, (who was with us at this reading) to get a tattoo of the McQ family crest, identical to the one Chris had on his arm. William took Chris' driver's license because Illinois has an age requirement of 18. Chris wanted it known that he loved it. Rebecca referred to a tattoo with wings on it. At first, we didn't get it but then we recalled that Chris' roommate and dear friend, Raul, posted on Facebook a tattoo with the Charging Buffalo Bills logo with wings and CJM 1-3-2016. C'mon, people that is amazing.

"Chris has a dog with him. It mothers him like another child. This reference was to our beloved Lab Casey. I know for a fact they are together again.

He's in Hawaii, Rebecca told us. As I've already said, that doesn't surprise me given his penchant for wearing Hawaiian shirts, even in the winter. We recently found a quote from Chris on twitter that stated "Hawaiian shirt going on, bad decisions to follow." He gets to be and do what he wants. Your Dad Joe is with him. He's in good hands. He said he will miss the other two kids. Rebecca told us Chris is an advanced spirit. And although he exited due to an accident he had a designated exit point the following year at 22. She said he finished his work early.

Rebecca then started giving us snippets from Chris (although he would never use that word). He sends us cardinals and is referring to a jacket. He is saying happy birthday to his cousin Charlie and, according to Rebecca, is jumping up and down. He's saying hi to his brother William. Rebecca said he is there with another William who he hangs out with. That could be my Uncle Bill or my brother Billy. Showing a flag (both served in the military). Chris said that his death was not intentional at all and that it was so sad. He said he didn't want to go. He told Rebecca we should get a second house. "It's a great idea," Chris said.

Rebecca said Chris is still the life of the party. And he's a prankster. He will reach us through all kinds of songs. He is so well respected and loved. My Dad has his hands on his shoulders. When your heart is open he will talk to you.

And then Rebecca moved on. She approached some other people hungering for a contact but it was all a blur. All I could think of was my Chris smiling on a beach on the other side.

What we were just part of feels like a psychic hurricane. It's so powerful and all encompassing... and then it's gone. There is an electric energy that carries you through the rest of the evening and then you're incredibly let down the next day. You expect it, but you never really get used to it. One particularly cool aspect of this visit was that we brought Chris' cousin Charlie along. They were close to the same age and both faced similar struggles. I had written earlier about Chris driving 16 straight hours from Chicago to Vermont, only to turn immediately around to escort Charlie to Wilderness. Although they didn't spend much time together as kids, despite living pretty close to one another, they were bound together by similar struggles, more than blood. Chris had been used to being of service to others in Tucson so when it came to family he truly rallied. Charlie was amazed. Not only did Chris come through, but he reached out directly to him, and wished him a happy birthday.

This visit was amazing. Rebecca was amazing. It seemed like she was talking with Chris for 45 minutes but I bet it was less than ten. No wonder Chris told Thomas John in December of 2016 referring to Sally seeing another medium. "You saw Rebecca …she's the real deal." And she truly is.

I want to go back to the Song "Live Like You Were Dying" by Tim McGraw. In August 2012 my buddies Brad, Aric, Jimmy Cohn and I flew to Tucson to put on a show for the Ranch Boys. Chris was working at the Ranch and living in an apartment with some pals. I rented this great house in Tucson with a huge patio, hot tub, grill, and water fall (really). It was a terrific set up. We decided to have a combo cook out and rehearsal on the patio. (Chris was coming over after work with his co-worker, Sam. When Chris arrived, the steaks were grilling and the sun was just setting. We enjoyed our feast and started to go through the next day's song list. Sam pulled out his guitar and joined in. He was so talented that we all just stopped and listened to his homemade music and ballads.

We convinced him to do a set with us the following day. One of the songs Brad started rehearsing for the show was "Live Like You Were Dying." I hadn't heard it before and it really touched my soul. The women who owned the house we were renting were sitting on the upstairs porch listening to the rehearsal. We knew we would be okay the next day when they broke into applause and cheers after our set. The next day at the ranch we were treated by Patrick to a wonderful cook out. We did a meeting with the boys and hit the stage. It was something I will always remember. We were standing on stage looking at the desert mountains in the distance as the sun set. When Brad started "Live Like You Were Dying" I looked out in the audience and saw Patrick sitting on a picnic bench visibly shaken. After the show I approached him and asked about his reaction. He told me that a dear friend of his who helped start the ranch had died of cancer and that was his favorite song. He felt his friend's spirit around him when we were performing. At the first Annual Chris McQ Golf Outing in September 2016 we performed that song and dedicated it to "someone who was like another father to Chris." Patrick was there in the audience feeling Chris around him. Obviously, that song means a lot to all of us. And after this, I hope to you.

I need to try to explain more clearly what Rebecca meant about designated exit points. According to Guy Needler, author and spiritual teacher, "Our souls have pre-planned not just one, but 3-5 exit points in every lifetime. It's the soul (not the ego) that gets to choose on the energetic level if and when to leave early." Kim Russo wrote about exit points in her book, *The Happy Medium.* In layman's terms, it appears that all of us have three to five pre-planned times when we are meant to leave our body. These are called exit points. What particularly resonated with me was Kim's point that if you had two NDE's, the third one is always an exit point. This really lines up. Chris rolled a pickup which was air born and he fell down a mineshaft where he was visited by an angel. But those occasions must not have been his time. But the third time is the one where he ran out of hall passes. According to Kim, this is what happens, it's just the deal

What Rebecca told us was that 22 years of age was Chris last exit point. If his soul didn't choose to leave on January 3, 2016, he would only have a limited time left on his soul contract.

This is how spiritual teacher Tanaaz Chubb defines a soul contract:

> *"Before you entered this physical time and space your soul made an agreement. Before you came into human form, your soul had specific purpose or destiny that it had agreed to fulfil. This destiny was written and is your Soul Contract.*
>
> *We all have Soul Contracts and essentially it is the list of lessons that we are meant to acquire in this life time in order to advance our soul to a higher level of consciousness"*

On the morning of February 25, 2017 at the usual time, after going through my pre-game routine, Chris came through. When I say came through I mean that thoughts are clearly coming into my mind after meditation. I am working on seeing him as the clairvoyants do but I have not been able to yet. Still, I am grateful for what I am given.

> *"Hi dad, I love you. We'll be together again. Red birds (cardinals) you see me. Love the tattoo, makes me laugh. Room for your spirit guide too, all the time in the world. It's me. I miss ya, dad. Hey dad, keep trying it will come. It works better when I am calling you. I'm around. Go deeper. See ya"*

There's so much packed into this short message. He refers to the tattoo that has to be Will's new family crest. He refers to cardinals which I believe is Chris' spirit when I see one. He tells me there is room for my spirit guide and I have no idea what that means. And he lets me know that the process works better when he is reaching out to me, instead of the other way around. That was true even when he was on this side too. The reference to the spirit guide and me not understanding it is just further confirmation that these thoughts didn't originate with me or I would understand all of them, which I don't always do. It's strange that being confused is validating, but in this case, it is.

My next visit with Chris was March 4, 2017. You need to understand that I feel Chris around me all the time. I especially feel him when I'm riding in my jeep listening to our music, playing golf where I talk to him and sitting on my Buffalo Bill's chair, next to his grave, cigar in hand. When 3 a.m. rolled around I was sitting at my desk surrounded by candles and sage burning. Chris came right through.

"Our time, pop. Work on this. Pick up tips. Like a golf lesson. I miss golfing with you. I miss you. It was very crowded at Rebecca's medium session. It will be a little less hectic with Thomas John in Wilmette. Glad you brought Charlie (to Rebecca's). Good call mom. (Sure, give her credit but I paid for the tickets). He'll be okay. He's just riding the wave. Taking what they are giving him. He'll wake up. It's warm and soft here."

"I loved the song Feathers. Glad you are redoing it in a slower rhythm. Energy…. try to figure that out. It's hard to imagine but look into it. You'll get it. I'm glad you visit the (grave). But better when it's warm. When you can just hang out and relax. More like when we hung out. Easy and Free like Fitz sang. Trust the process and trust the pen. Get it? Like falling asleep. You're not

imagining this. Feel me around you. Energy. We're together like in Scottsdale. Or hanging on the same bed watching the Bill's game before I crossed. I LOVED THAT TOO! I know how much you did. We can still do that…Energy. Wake back up pop, I'm with you. Let go like falling into sleep. Like a slow water slide. You still make me happy pop. We'll be together again. Trust it. Don't forget to look for me. I'm not wasting my time, it's for you…look. No glow on candle. I'm here. Now you got it. Pat's here. We crossed together. Believe it.

Gotta go…see you… love you."

Chris really has a way of saying a lot in a short visit. He gives me great advice about picking up tips from different sources. He said Rebecca's session was crowded. Although there were perhaps 100 guests at the event, what he meant that it was crowded with spirits. We have been told that the loved ones who cross keep their same personality. If you were shy on this side, you will display that trait on the other side. And conversely, if you were a strong personality in this life, you will be forceful in the other. That's why we shouldn't be surprised when Chris always makes his way through, even in a crowded venue. He was and always will be a force to be reckoned with. That really makes me proud to be his father.

He referred to us bringing his cousin Charlie to Rebecca's reading. In fact, Charlie had been a bit lost and unfocused for a while and now, as Chris predicted, he is finding his focus and his drive. Chris talked about the song we wrote "I'll Send You Feathers" and said he liked that we were slowing it down. Right after this session Brad went back into the studio and in fact slowed it down. It seems important that I push to try to figure out energy. I can only assume it's the key to connecting. Chris telling me that he likes my graveside visits and that is reassuring. Chris' liking the visits more when it's warm is so him. It's also much nicer to sit and talk when the sun is shining and I can feel the warmth around me, just as we hung out together. *"Easy and free like Fitz's song."* The first St. Patty's day after Chris' passing was a mere ten weeks later. I went to Libertyville to see my pal Paul Fitzpatrick and his band Fitz & the Celts play.

Between sets Fitz picked up a guitar and announced he was dedicating the next song to a fine young Irishman who was gone too soon. He dedicated "I'm a Man You Don't Meet Every Day" to my boy.

I knew at the time Chris loved it. And here a year later he was referring to how perfect the lyrics were. Paul Fitz has been a source of support and love through his friendship and music. He plays in Frat Dog at Chris' annual golf outing and my world is a better place because of Paul.

Chris referred to us being next to one another at various times and places. I loved nothing better than lying near my sleeping boy. I miss that more than I can say.

He also reinforces that we will be together again. It's so loving the way he soothes my heart with that message. He closed with the message that Pat, the one boy out of the three who drowned with Chris who we knew and loved was with him, and okay. He tells me to believe it and I do.

On March 10, 2017 we had an appointment at 6 p.m. to be part of a Spirit Circle with Thomas John, the medium who connected with Chris at the Wilmette Theatre. On that morning Chris woke me up and I started the process. Pretty soon, I felt the tingle on my neck and knew he was around.

"Hey Dad, It's warm here. Always warm and clean. Tropical flower smells. It's okay, the block is just a learning curve. Like

a learning disorder what I don't have anymore." (not grammat-
ically correct but the way it came through) "It's great to be able
to look at something and figure it out- almost anything. Smartest
guy around now ☺." "Don't get caught up. It's all about flow.
You'll get it. I'm teaching you. Pretty cool, right. Reminds me of
you and me with history. Well, now I know. I'll be there tonight
to insure mom and Will know it's all about love. To teach them
enlightenment. Them and you Dad.

It's a short run dad. Mine shorter than yours but don't get
bogged down. Over there it's really nothing. It seems so important
but it's not. Stay in the spirit Pops. Don't drift to worldly problems.
I can help. I'm kind of like an Angel for you (not officially). But
they are around you and always have been. You felt them on the
beach when you were lost and needed them. Always there, you
just didn't know. Lots of stuff like that. You just need to awaken
more- Blessed.

I miss you too Pop, I know it hurts but don't stay in the
pain. Soon enough old man- you and me again. This is our time
Pop. You feel me now, don't you? Can't deny me being around
you. Nothing between us- just us. Just the way I like it remember.
You brought me comfort and made me safe. I never knew I did
the same for you until now.

Don't cry, I'm close to you. It's all good. Just relax and let
me help you now. Every day Pop. Stay close to my friends. God,
how I loved them and still do. They are healing, Pop not moving
on. I trust their love for me completely. But they can't stay in the
loss forever- you too.

It's real-it's real. I'm real. This world is real.

See Ya Pop… I love you. Clear your head now, clear your heart."

That visit with Chris was almost a year ago. Everything I write about each visit comes directly from my notes. But sometimes when reading those notes it feels like I'm seeing them for the first time. The message is so clear and the words are so much like the way Chris talked that any doubts I had have completely disappeared. I have been given an extraordinary gift of being to stay in contact with my precious son, on his terms, of course. But that is no different than how it was on this side.

I'm amazed at how much he says in just a few paragraphs. He refers to helping me, with the learning curve of communicating with him on the other side. He talks about a learning disability that was part of life on this side not existing anymore. He likes being the smartest guy around which fills my heart with joy. When he was a leader on the Ranch in Tucson, he was looked up to, and that filled him with pride. Nothing could make me happier. He knew we were seeing Thomas John tonight and let me know he would be there. He is hammering home that things on this side aren't really that important, so don't get bogged down and that he would be there to help get me through. He also referred to angels on the beach which I've already mentioned. I was having a particularly hard time in business and the fear flowed into every aspect of my life. On a spring break in Naples Fla., I took a walk on Vanderbilt Beach at night and felt a tingling on the back of my neck and a sense of wellness flowed over me. I somehow knew it was angels sending me peace. I got through that period and held on to the knowing. It was a precursor to my search for the other side. Chris let me know there is nothing between us now. It's just like when he was a kid and would jump up on the bed and I would say, "Well pal I guess it's just you and me," and he would respond, "Yep, just the way I like it." Forgive me if I have said this already. But it is a very precious memory and it gets me through some pretty dark times.

I guess I was starting to fret that his pals were starting to move on. When Sally asked me if I thought they were starting to forget about him I told her absolutely not. But in my heart, I guess that fear was sinking in.

Chris let me know that he loved and still loves them and that they were healing rather than moving on. I had nothing to worry about. The following summer we met with his NIU pals several times at his grave and then had lunch at a local burger joint. I know Chris was beaming. At least a dozen of those pals joined us at his golf outing in September and we had more than 40 people at his grave on the second anniversary of his crossing 1/3/18. Most of those in attendance were NIU and New Trier pals. (Did I mention how much I friggin love those kids? I may have.) Chris also confirmed how real his world and our connection is. How could I possibly doubt it?

This was shaping up to be a pretty cool day spiritually. I had a heartwarming and somewhat breakthrough session with my boy and we will get to experience Thomas John at 6 p.m. in a spirit session or small group setting.

Actually, I really don't like small group readings. The energy of the group has a lot to do with the session. First of all, Thomas was late because he had a head cold. He had cancelled a session the day before but he felt he was going to be well enough to proceed. I had mixed feelings. I desperately wanted a small session with the medium who had knocked my socks off at Wilmette Theatre, but I know from my limited experience that a head cold can block the flow of messages. It actually happened to me in a writing session. So, I was cautiously optimistic that this would come off. I was there with Sally and Will. Will had a great reading with Andrew Anderson so I expected Thomas to really help him with his grief.

Well, Thomas was late and he did not seem as on his game as before. Once again, the problem with a small group is just that – it is a small group. The group was comprised of my family, a woman who lost her parents, another couple who lost a child and another couple consisting of a woman and a man that she dragged with her. He sat there with his arms crossed resenting his spouse, Thomas, and us all. It was really uncomfortable. When Chris was coming through after a pretty impressive string of connected messages, Thomas asked who's Karen. She's there with him. What he meant was Kerry, a cousin who is on the other side who had helped Chris cross according to basically every medium we had ever encountered. Although Thomas was addressing us, what we got was a chorus of comments from the magpies around the circle. All their chatter broke the stream, at least temporarily. What I wanted to yell was shush, you morons, he will get to you, but what I did was make a mental note about spirit circles. I like spirits better than most people.

In the session I got very little from Chris, which was disappointing and pretty unusual. I concluded that the session was flawed from congestion, or energy of the crowd. However, when I reviewed my notes and listened to the recording of the reading, I realized there were definitely messages from Christopher. They we strong and clear. How did I miss them? Well, they weren't for me. They were for his mom. In my self-centered mind it was a flop. I got a little but the majority was for his beloved mom, and because I was in the reading I will happily report what our boy said. The reading opened up with Sally's dad coming through.

Thomas told Sally that "Your father's coming through. He was pretty self-involved." He said he missed the opportunity to be a better father. Thomas stated there was a big divide between them and that Warren is very sorry. Thomas asked Sally, "Did he favor the boys? "That was a bit of an understatement. Thomas said that "frankly he was a little pissed off you weren't a boy".

I do love the no filter aspect of a good medium. He described Warren's office, their relationship and Warren himself to a T. He hasn't evolved much on the other side Thomas told us.

So now we start to hear from Chris. In hindsight, I feel like an ungrateful tool once I can see what has come through. Thomas told Will that Chris is really happy. "Your brother is the life of the party. He told us that a lot of people loved him and he had a lot of friends. Thomas asked us "How did he connect to a dog named Cooper?" Holy cow! Cooper is the Japanese Chin dog that Chris posed with all the time. Chris kept a blog for him and we named our band "Frat Dog" after him. (in case you forgot). Although he passed suddenly Thomas told us he had a really good life. He knew he was loved and appreciated. Chris always wanted to have a good time. Chris told Thomas he was on vacation (Christmas break) when he crossed. During that time, he spent a lot of time with friends and family and that he was very happy. Thomas told us more than one soul crossed with him. (see what I mean, a very disappointing reading ...duh)

He was laughing at his mom's search for perfect employment. He told her, "I'll help you find your purpose." He mentioned addiction, but that was separate from his passing. He's with Kerry (no not Karen, now sit down). He said he knew that Caroline was away and that she was in France. We told him she was in Spain, but then remembered she was recently in Paris visiting her God Mother, Anne. Thomas is right "never argue with a dead person." (It's the title of his book.)

When Chris first crossed over he thought, "Oh Fuck!" Thomas said. He never considered the possible consequences of his recklessness. When he first passed he felt a lot of regret over that but Thomas told us he has since forgiven himself. Thomas heard the song "When the Saints Go Marching In" playing, which was played exiting his funeral and sung by the McQ family as it was our old Parish's theme song from Buffalo. A song near to all of our hearts. "Does someone pour a beer over his grave? "asked Thomas. Only every time the Northern U kids come to visit him. Thomas said there is "lots of love for Sally from Chris." Thomas told us that Greek life (frat life) was a big deal to Chris. He knows his mom was conflicted about his life style and sends a nurse sign to signify that she always took care of him.

He said he loved to golf and told Thomas we have his clubs (which I do). Chris told Thomas that we recently connected with him through another medium. Chris came through to Rebecca Rosen on February 23.

Thomas did tell me (about friggin' time) that I am open and connect with Chris all the time. I asked Thomas if my dad is with Chris and he repeated that Chris came through another medium recently (with the following left unsaid...and she just told you that, didn't she, stupid?)

William asked Thomas why his mom and dad could connect and he really didn't. Thomas said we were more open and said that it will happen more for him when he's older. He also told Will that Chris had come to him in his dreams. Will wanted some proof and asked for some confirmation or a sign. In his mind and revealed to me he wanted Chris to mention the Buffalo Bills. Maybe it was Thomas' head cold or the pressure on Chris to name a specific team on the spot, but nothing came. That is until a private reading I had with Thomas on August 13th when he opens with, "Why is he showing me Marv Levy? "and at the same reading Thomas asked Sally, "Why do I see a charging Buffalo?" I truly believe this was in response to William's request for a sign about the Buffalo Bills. It might be five months late but that was Chris for you. He's on his own timetable even in the afterlife.

What I did learn from this experience is how important it is to record readings. Although I like taking notes, I don't want to lose the direct connection with the medium if I'm caught up in writing down every detail. There are subtle nuances in the medium's appearance and demeanor that are truly amazing. Andrew Anderson looks over your shoulder and makes a direct visual connection. Thomas squints and his eyes sort of roll back as he talks directly to the spirit. He's more than happy to interrupt you or his own train of thought when a spirit wants to make a point. "Uh huh, yeah, hmm okay" is Thomas verbally connecting with the spirit. It's really wonderful to be in the same space with the spirit to whom you are being connected. I love knowing that Chris is right behind me in a reading. Andrew has told me that in a group Chris is often behind me with his arms crossed resting on my head. I've seen Andrew smile directly over me, saying that Chris just kissed the top of my head. I have beamed as every medium has expressed how beautiful my son is. I am told he looks the same as when he crossed. Every medium has also touched on other aspects of my boy that also rang true. He's good-looking, fun loving, sweet, reckless, and charming. They have also told me that there was addiction, sadness, depression and regret at causing us so much pain, though it was unintentional.

I'm brutally honest in admitting that Chris died because of recklessness that certainly involved both drugs and alcohol. However, it's also important that you know that Chris didn't commit suicide. That fact is very important to Chris. Four sweet inebriated reckless boys jumped in a canoe in January and it ended tragically. I have known and have been told by mediums that Chris had thought about suicide in some dark times. But that was not the case on this cold January morning. He was happy and full of promise and life when he crossed. Recently, I was at an AA meeting with Rick, a good friend, who was speaking. After all the comments, the chairperson referred to he and I losing a child to suicide. It is unusual to interrupt or talk out of turn but I did just that. I set the record straight by telling the group that Chris died tragically and alcohol certainly played a part. But he didn't take his life. It's important that you know that. Chris has made it clear that's it's vital to him that we know that. Thoughts of suicide are not that uncommon in people who have alcohol problems, even when they're sober. I am certainly not the same guy who walked in the doors of AA in 1985. As a parent who has lost a child I will match my emotional grief and pain against anyone's. However, if your child commits suicide you endure additional pain from the guilt that you were unable to prevent the suicide. I have beaten myself up pretty well regarding things I wish I had done, done differently or not done at all involving Chris. I can't imagine the torment that is layered on top of that when a child commits suicide. I think I just got a message to add parents' surviving their kid's suicide to the list of my prayers (that list is usually reserved for me and my family...selfish guy that I am).

Thomas mentioned that frat life was important to Chris. That was so true. As I have mentioned, Chris was a pretty bad student. Yet in a conversation with his Uncle Mike Holmberg, he recited the entire Greek lineage of presidents and events. He was beaming with pride as was his godfather when Chris shared these details. Chris went on to become pledge master and I believe he expected to become chapter president the following year. His involvement with the fraternity was great for his self-esteem and spirt.

On March 15, I met with Andrew Anderson. He had become a bit of a pal as well as conduit to talk to my boy. He told me Chris knew we were planning a trip abroad. He said that Chris would travel with us and come to me in Spain. He mentioned that Chris was such handsome guy. Look for his spirit at an old church or cemetery. He told me I would feel a déjà vu, and that I should research *psychic impressions*. We had a connection to Spain. Chris said that Caroline is struggling but will come around. Chris said it is difficult for her as she was always in Chris' shadow. Even now there is a lot of attention on the other side. Thomas reinforced that the time Chris comes to me between 3 a.m. and 4 a.m. This is reportedly the time of most spirit activity. Andrew confirmed that it's Chris communicating with me; he is helped by my Dad and brother Jerry. He said Chris feels that Florida is a spiritual place for me.

The jargon used by the mediums is still new to me so I had to google "psychic impression."

Here is what a *psychic impression* is from the Master Shift

Your Soul and Spirit will speak to you in whatever ways they can reach you. They will use your vocabulary, frame of reference, experiences, and even your humor. How else would you recognize the messages they are sending you?

You receive spiritual communication, guidance, and information from your Soul and Divine Spirit through one or more of your six psychic senses.

We all have some degree of psychic sensitivity whether we are aware of it or not. Some have more abilities than others. Your psychic abilities can improve and expand if you learn more about them and if you practice using them.

One of the ways your Soul and Spirit will guide and support you in life is through psychic impressions.

You may psychically hear sentences or words that come to you usually as a thought, rather than as an actual sound. The words may seem like they are in your voice or in someone else's voice. They may be faint or loud.

You may psychically get a gut feeling of what to say or do. You may sense the aches, challenges, and personalities of others. You may sense the presence of guides, deceased loved ones, and angels. This is usually the strongest and easiest way for most people to receive guidance.

You may psychically know information, ideas, and understanding that just come to you without pictures or words. You know that it is important. You pay attention.

You may psychically see pictures flash in your mind's inner third eye as in-sights or outside of you. They may be a still photo, a movie, or a life-like scene. When the image is of a psychic origin and you aren't thinking it up yourself, the image is seen first and then thought about afterwards. That's how you know you can trust it and that you're not making it up because it comes to you.

You may psychically taste a substance, liquid, or food without actually putting anything in your mouth.

You may also psychically smell fragrance, flowers, food, or tobacco even when the substance is not in your surroundings.

Don't be afraid. There is a sense of love, peace, comfort, empowerment, and happiness when you are truly connecting with your Soul and Divine Spirit.

You often connect naturally with psychic impressions when you sleep, daydream, do something creative, commune with nature, walk, meditate, or are mindful. Be sure to practice these things often to develop your psychic sensitivity.

Remember to look, listen, and feel the psychic impressions that are all around you.

All the good mediums have told me that I won't need them to connect with Chris as I evolve and practice. Still, even though I can reach my son while meditating, I still hunger for the clear direct connection a truly great medium provides. I want to look in his eyes as he communicates with my son. I want to view him seeing my boy. There is something truly spiritually humbling about being part of a world that I once never even considered.

I stumbled on this reading from John 16:16 while researching something else.

Jesus told his disciples, "For a little while you won't see me, but after a while you will see me."

You may say that mediums are "new age" but we've always been able to communicate with those who have passed over. They are with us and we can see them if we work at it.

CHAPTER TEN:

You Can Do Hard

On March 23, 2017 Chris woke me up and after the normal rituals of the candles, sage, chakra tune up and meditation came through. Sometimes I listen to a guided meditation and sometime just the meditation music. That's the routine.

"Hi Dad, my friends are rallying and still remember. I told you they would. It was real love. I didn't give for no reason. The love went both ways. I'm glad you get it now. I would do the same for any one of them. Both ways. Get it? Always warm, always calm…nice.

Just be there for Will. He'll come around. He needs to know you love him as much as you loved me…. And I know, you know how much you loved me. Even when it wasn't easy the love was always there. And I hung onto it like a rung on a fire escape. (Metal bars on a cement wall) it's a visual- see it. Lots of visuals to explain this. All energy. You are getting there. No need to rush it. It will come when you are ready. We have forever to figure it out together. White Power Ranger (see a visual). Relax, it's in the cards; it's fine. I wish we could be together like before. But it won't be that long. It will be better (which is not easy to be).

Andrew's right, I'm still good looking. Always have been. It's my energy trade mark- and kind. Even if I was reckless. (I'll tell you something, I still am.) Just no danger. Still pushing limits. Like visiting you Pop."

"See I told you it was work getting out of bed. (getting your ass out of bed). Gonna be spring soon and you and I can golf together. I'm with you every time. You feel me. Its pure fun with you…my guy. Keep searching for sea shells. Right mom. She loved that in Florida. She was really happy then. Get back to that joy momma…. I'm here with you. I just needed to figure out how to get back to you. But I did it. And did it quickly. I'm very smart now. Meditation Dad is the key to this. Let go, let God, let go. Feels like floating. I'm showing you this side like I showed you guys the Ranch. I knew every rock and tree. Same here. My place that we will share. It's all good. Love those boys, they loved me, love me, they still do and I feel it all. Their love, your love, mom's love. No limits. It's huge over here. Wait til you see it. It will blow your mind."

"Kind of talkative today, huh? Lots of energy and freedom- Wow it's great, really kind of like heaven (just kidding it's what you know as heaven). More you and less a God. We are all God-energy, right- love. Glad you are putting my stuff back on the grave. But glad for you, not for me. I don't need it. Only need you there. Only need you on your side. Think about surfing, now think about air. Blows your mind, right?"

"No regrets. Don't miss it. Too nice here. But love you guys. As close to missing as I can. Doesn't mean I don't love you, but hard to miss the work where you are. A cosmic vacation. Think surfing. Good meditation music today. Not for me, for you. I don't have A.D.D. any more but you do ☺. You're hanging in Pop. You always feel a letdown after these but it's worth it.

I love to talk to you without having to talk. It's real."

Done
Love yu
C Boy

This conversation needs no interpretation or explanation. It's massive in its spiritual content. This reading was just a pure gift of love from my wonderful son.

On April 1, I got a short visit from Chris.

"I love you too pop. I was with you the other night but you can feel me, now right? Let it go, flowing like a river. Like Niagara, in Canada with the family. The twins. We are all connected. They are a good example, but we are all connected. You're caught up in events of one day. Let them go. I'm smiling at you."

Then he was gone again.

Chris referred to Canada and the twins. Every August we join my family for a weeklong reunion in Crystal Beach, Ontario. We've been doing it now for over 10 years. There's lots of beach time, golf, tennis and general chicanery. I can't put my finger on it but we all have a ball. One of my joys upon arrival was watching Chris team up with his twin cousins Matt and David. They merged into one unit and didn't separate for a week. God it made my heart burst with joy. Chris loved being a McQuillen and loved being surrounded and accepted by the clan. The first August back after Christopher crossed over was a heartbreaking time for us all, and we left early. It was somehow too lonely without him. I would see three tow-headed boys walking astride toward the beach and my heart would break a little and I would begin to cry. Loving someone that much does have its price tag.

In April, Sally and I took a week to join our Caroline in Spain. She had left for a semester abroad in January, and although it was a great opportunity for her on so many levels we missed her terribly. On the night of April 9, on a hotel balcony in Madrid,

Chris pulled a drive by. It was just a short visit to touch base as Andrew said he would. It was a beautiful moonlight night and I was pulled out to the balcony with a legal pad and a pen. I meditated and called on Chris to visit.

> *"Hi Pop, it's me. Florida, Spain, Winnetka, I'm here. It's all one world. All the same, get it? Glad you got up. This is truly our time, and at the grave. Doing fine and watching over you. My pals are getting together to celebrate my birthday. I'll be there, every step. Around them and loving them. Stay close to them. My spirit is in them too."*
>
> *"I know you miss me but it won't be that long. And I'm always around you. Pay attention. It's always me. Short visit but look for me on the coast. I love the coast. Love you guys."*

April 15 was Christopher's 23rd birthday. We were flying home from visiting Caroline in Spain so I didn't have a chance to tap into his energy. We landed in the afternoon which gave me just enough time to drop off my suitcase at home, take a quick hot tub, change and head to Naperville where Chris' pals were sponsoring a pub crawl in honor of his birthday. There were more than 100 participants in one of Chris' favorite pastimes. I was able to get to the first stop just as it was kicking off. I bought a whole lot of pitchers and did a whole lot of hugging. William had been hanging out with Chris' pals all afternoon and joined the revelry. After a couple of hours Will and I slipped out and made our way back toward home. I had one stop to make however to keep the birthday tradition alive. Sally met me at Sacred Heart Cemetery and we floated a Chinese lantern up to our boy as the darkness fell. This time we grieved together with our emotion flooding over us both. How could one boy have such complete possession of both of our hearts?

On April 19. I sat at my desk at the witching hour after my ritual and got nothing. I guess he was busy. Oh well, back to bed. I wonder if a *Law and Order* rerun is on...

On April 25, we had a visit.

"I'm not going away. You felt me when mom read the prologue to her book." (Sally is writing a book about raising Chris.) "I'm around you. It ebbs and flows like the tide. I came to Caroline so she knows I'm still here. Now you're getting it, Pops, now it's flowing. William needs guidance- keep pushing. I'm here, Pop. I'm not going anywhere, trust it. Work on your end...do your part. Get proficient as a conduit, a voice. How can you question after all of this? When you get caught up on things on your side, it's hard to connect. Don't worry about it. Go deeper. You can do hard, Remember. Tell momma I love her book (you will too)."

"I loved my friends and my life. But this is truly where I belong. This is my world. I tried to make the other world work, but it's home here. You'll see, you'll get it."

"Think about the best brochure on line for the greatest tropical resort and it's even better. That's here, Pop. You will love it. And I will be here for you. Sometimes I'm a young kid but mostly I'm my age, 21. I was in my prime. Awkward as a kid and older wasn't in the cards. I'm really content. I'm really okay with it. Except for your and momma's pain. I feel that and I'm sorry. But you know that I can't help it now.

Make your peace with the gulf warm beaches. Can you hear the surf? That's my every day. What's not to like? It's good here, honest. Just keep going. You'll find your way. Eventually you'll find your way here. You feel me, now Pops?"

"Tell mom I love her. She was the one. Tell her that. She'll know what it means. We had a connection. It was deep, it was

spiritual, and it was real. Tell her to believe that. Don't ever doubt that. She was my go-to. Always love."

"Walk on the warm beaches at night. Warm waves reaching up to my feet. Always awesome.

Go to bed, Pop."
Love you so much

Almost a year later I am reading this exchange and I am amazed at its clarity. Things about our relationship and his friends. About what age he is on the other side. Things I hadn't considered. Even his pushing me to go further and go deeper. Chris said, "You can do hard" and prompted me to remember. When he was at the ranch on the first family visit, we met in a group. Chris stated that one emotional exercise was hard. One of the counselors quoted a wilderness therapist and responded, "Chris, you can do hard." When the grief is sometimes almost unbearable I think back and recall "you can do hard." Because boy it's friggin hard. This visit was so powerful I had to reread the message to Sally about her being the one. We both began to cry… but we can do hard. And we are so very grateful to Christopher's continued commitment to us.

On April 27, I had a reading with Andrew Anderson. I decided to try something a little different with Andrew and just ask a few questions of Chris. I would ask the question and Andrew would look over my shoulder in that *medium way* and respond (or not).

Here is how it went. Some responses are first person and some are Andrew answering for Chris.

Q: Chris are you pulling way …

A: No response or having responded to this over and over in the past; maybe he chose not to respond. (can spirits roll their eyes)

Q: Do you wake me up or is it me waking up and you show up?

A: Chris says he wakes you up

Q: Did you visit Caroline in Majorca (Spain)? She said you came to her in a dream carrying a big rock over your head.

A: Yes

Q: Are you planning on meeting Marcia when she crosses? Are Jerry and Pat going to be there also?

A: He will be the first to meet her.

Q: Do you see Jerry on your side? Are you close?

A: Jerry and my Dad

I asked the next two questions and got one response. So, I'm not sure if the answer covered both questions or he chose to answer one (in the middle of it your mind is in a bit of a fog even as the recipient of a reading). You can't really ask for clarification and I am just so grateful for the contact that I don't want to seem greedy.

Q: Do you see my Dad? What does he have to say to you?

Q: I'm having trouble around staying on the In Balance Ranch Charity Board? What do you think?

A: Stop Doubting

Q: What can I do to stay as close as the air to you? Love you

A: Signs

That was the extent of question and answer period. Chris started sending messages of his own.

Chris said he likes that I find things (signs). Maybe in response to my very first question. Chris said, "I'm devoting more time with other family members."

Chris told Andrew "William was recently playing poker with Chris' pals." Chris showed Andrew a ring. Andrew said I should look to a ring. Chris reconfirmed that he is with my brother Jerry and my Dad.

To William, Chris said "Mom and dad don't need the added pressure…get your butt back to school."

Chris stated "Finding Christopher…write it Pop." Andrew described seeing Chris sitting on a stone bench with his arm around me. Andrew said he saw Chris bringing me to a party. Maybe it was Chris showing me he was at his birthday celebration with me.

Chris said he "tried to take Marcia to the other side in a dream" "It's okay, Dad…I'm here."

On May 9, Chris came through to me. I was going to fold over a picture of Chris and his dear pal Mish, not because I don't love her, but rather because I thought it would help me focus on his spirit. Mish was not just a close friend and confidant but another mother to my boy. She would help take care of him, when events weren't bad enough for his real mom to step in. Sally and I adore her. She is truly part of our family.

"Leave her in Pop… you know I loved her and still love her. All one. Get it. You sure have been a little quiet or a little dormant. But it seems to have been awakened. Maybe it's spring. Love the music and the new book. Tell Brad thanks. He really is giving of himself and digging deep. What a good guy he is. I'm glad you are close right now. It's warm and cool here. It's hard to explain but it's like when the day is over and is turning into the soft night. Really nice. Really quiet. I was with you and Uncle Mike at the grave on Sunday. Lying next to you guys. That was nice. It was about me and was humble and sweet."

"Momma's birthday (coming up). Make it nice. She'll hear from me. Tell her to meditate before the reading. Tell her to take the time to immerse herself in my world, our world. Jerry says hi. Cassidy sees me all the time. She doesn't know any difference. My presence makes her feel safe. I visit her when you guys are gone. Just her and me. My roommate …remember?

Let go of the mineshaft stuff. It would not have mattered. I had a path and I'm glad to be home. Miss you though."

"I visited Caroline. I told you I'd visit you on the coast. I should have been more specific. I saw her on the coast. Don't worry. It all will work out. I'm getting things done on this side to help. It's like when you get things done on your side. Like father, like son, Dad. It's all fine. Love mom more, I sure do. I can feel her spirit, her love, her momma thing all the way here. (not really that far). Glad you got your ass up. I missed this. You were drifting not me, Dad.

Trust I'm always around you until you come home. Trust it. Back of the neck Pops, feel it?

Do the bird thing(tattoo) It makes me smile."

"Just love Will. Fuck everything else. School, counseling, etc. Just love him. He'll come through it. He is sick. Get the blood test.

He's not faking. Dude, way to hang in there. Loving this. Good start to my day. My days are long and sweet and warm. How could you write if I'm not around you? So quit doubting. Just love me and I'll just love you. Like always. I always knew you loved me like crazy. I sometimes took it for granted. But not now. I can feel it from your soul and I love you. Make the book a priority. It will actually be a success, and I'll be around digging it all, loving it all. Glad you're here in our world between worlds. Go downstairs and look up at the sky, at the stars and I will too. Different from here, though. Tell my momma I'll be with her all day on her birthday. Tell her to get quiet and love and feel and don't be sad. I'm still with her like when I was just a kid… her and me."

Night Dad, I love you.

Ps remember Brad Paisleys Letter to Me… this is my letter to you

As usual this visit doesn't need a lot of explanation or interpreting. He wanted me to let go of the mineshaft incident. Although I was with him in Scottsdale, after the fall, and nursed him at home, he could have used counseling for the emotional trauma. Patrick Barrasso, from the Ranch, offered to arrange and even pay for it. I presented the offer to Chris and he dismissed it. However, as his dad, I should have known better and insisted. But I didn't, and that has haunted me. Maybe things would have taken a different path. But Chris is telling me there is only one path. Maybe it's true. Or maybe he is just lovingly trying to let his old man off the hook.

Another message from Chris was that his brother Will was having a hard time and started down a path that has since been corrected. He's been accepted at Boulder, which was his first choice. And although he's in an alternative school his grades are fine. He will begin club lacrosse in a few weeks and he seems okay. I think Chris has been helping, a lot.

Chris told me he liked the Cardinal tattoo idea. I did get a tattoo on my arm, but it was a feather with his name under it. Upon further review I think there is a Cardinal tattoo in my near future. He closes with reference to a song he loved and turned me on to. So dear reader …listen to me. Put down the book and copy and paste https://youtu.be/RQ3bn7V0zdU *Letter to Me, by Brad Paisley.*

Close your eyes and listen. Then thank Chris for bringing the song to you.

(Authors update I did get the cardinal tattoo a year later on May 14, 2018, and it makes my heart sing)

Chris' next visit was May 21.

"I'm here…still here. I'm like yelling so you get it. You are so afraid that I'm drifting away that you are missing me every day. I'm not missing out. I can do my things and still be with you all the time. In the Jeep, at the grave on the beach. It's the deal. I can be doing both. You're not pulling me out of something to be with you. I love you and love being around you. I will always be there until we are together again. Until you cross and then together again on the other side. It's a soul thing. Find out about the soul; it's who we are. Stay on the track of that. Pure love, pure love. Always warm and happy. It's a good deal pop. Now you get it. Feeling me on the back of your neck. I love the book idea. Stay on the visits. It's what people need to feel, to see, to believe. I'm glad it's you and me bringing this stuff out together. Short visit but intense. A lot has been said before. Go through the notes. Higher energy, lots of fast soft movement. Nothing is harsh, always smooth. Even when

I zoom around it's really soft and warm. Kind of a theme here. Nothing to be afraid of. Let go, let it all go. Don't get caught up in other people's reality. This is our reality and I'm running this for us. I know what I'm doing. Trust me. Like when I'd show you around Tucson. It was my world and you were happy to let go. Proud I knew the way. That's how this is but you gotta trust me. Trust God. Trust you to let go and float Dad. There you go - getting closer.

You need new candles. Get them today. Good for the focus and you need that bad. (psychic joke from your boy). Smiling at you. Glad the dog is here. I love her and miss her in the flesh but see her in my spirit. She is pure love. That's the thing about animals. Trust and love.

Smell me dad. It's me. Don't listen to anyone. I've worked hard to be able to sit with you. Don't doubt it. Don't fuck it up. New level of meditation. Lean back and just envision me and I will become more whole to you. Do it now. Coming through the glass wall at American Airlines, running to you when you came home from work. Same me, same love. It's my gift to you, truly. I'm proud of you dad. You're starting to get it. Fight through any doubt, any lack of faith. It's me. Love you so much. Pure love to you Dad. It hurts but it's a good hurt. A connected hurt. It's a promise we will be connected on the other side. As soon as you fall you will see me walking toward you with a smile. You were my rock and I will be yours- love the shift. You can make the shift just fine.

Worth getting out of bed for isn't it? My time between 3 and 4, our time. It scares you to get this close to the other side. Let it go. Keep working on it. I'm proud of you Dad, that's what Rebecca (Rosen) told mom. Just proud and love you."

Gotta Jump
Love you-

This was an amazing visit on so many levels. My notes about Chris coming through the glass wall at American Airlines as a young man when he came back from Tucson, or when he ran to me when I came home from work at night as a kid, took me back to those sweet days. That in itself was a gift. I only had 21 years of him on this side, but no father was ever more grateful for his son's pure love. I am so grateful that I am still the recipient of his love through the veil. One of the things that confirms to me the messages are from Chris is that in one instance he is dead wrong. In no way does my connection to the other side scare me. What scares me is the thought of somehow losing that. Chris continues to insist that won't happen. It's strange that a misread on his part is truly an affirmation to me that it's all real, and not just a grieving father's imagination. (I knew you were thinking that.)

I smile when he asks or really tells me that I can smell him. I can smell that sweet smell of sweat that lingers on active young men. It could be the sage, but I think it's more. But that's just me. You will need to decide for yourself. But give yourself or your loved on the other side a chance before you decide.

This is a good time to try to explain the difference between a soul and spirit. This definition comes from *Answers about the Afterlife: A Private Investigator's 15-Year Research Unlocks the Mysteries of Life after Death* by Bob Olson. It may take a little while to wrap your hands around his message but it's worth reading.

What is the difference between a soul and a spirit? It would be difficult for you to understand some of the answers in this book without an initial understanding of my definitions for the word's 'soul' and 'spirit.' Based on the evidence I've seen, this is how I perceive the relationship between soul and spirit. You don't have to fully understand or accept my definitions at this point, but it'll help you to understand my answers throughout this book. The soul is our whole self, the eternal and spiritual aspect of who we are. Since I've seen evidence that we experience many human lives, the soul is what is experiencing all those lifetimes. So, if my soul has had a lifetime as Bob, another lifetime as George, and another lifetime as Sarah, then Bob, George, and Sarah all come from the same soul. I like to explain this using the analogy of the ocean and its waves. First, there is the ocean, then from that ocean come the waves. The ocean is the soul, and the waves are the spirits—in this case, the spirit of Bob, the spirit of George, and the spirit of Sarah. So, Bob, George, and Sarah are like waves, and their soul is like the ocean. Each spirit has its own individual characteristics, but each will also have some common characteristics of its soul. Because of this, another soul will always be able to recognize a spirit's soul identity because of those signature characteristics. In other words, my wife's soul will always be able to recognize my soul regardless of what life it is experiencing. Said another way, if we could watch videos of Bob, George, and Sarah, we would be able to recognize similarities among them, which would be these signature characteristics of their soul. We might recognize their soul in their eyes, their voice, or their mannerisms, but we'd recognize it for sure. Now taking this a step further, when I die, my spirit as Bob will leave my physical body and return home to the spirit world. In essence, my spirit will rejoin my soul and remain as an eternal aspect of my soul. In the same way that my human personality as a teenager is always present within me as an adult, my spirit as Bob will always be present in my soul. To keep the comparison going, Bob as a young boy, Bob as a teenager, Bob as a young adult, Bob as a middle-aged adult, and—if I live that long—Bob as an older adult are all different human aspects of my life as Bob, just as the spirit of Bob, the spirit of George, and the spirit of Sarah are all different aspects of my soul. You've probably heard people talk about their inner child. Well, there's also an inner teenager,

inner young adult, and inner middle-aged adult as well. These
are parts of me that never disappear even though I age and my
appearance and personality change a little. So, the equivalent to
any of these inner aspects of myself would be my soul's inner Bob,
inner George, or inner Sarah. While the spirits of Bob, George,
and Sarah returned to the spirit world, thereby rejoining my soul
(their whole self), their individual essences always remain as part
of that soul. Hence, they too do not disappear, meaning that I
can always communicate with my father, who is in spirit, or my
grandmother. It's not as if they disappear into their souls either.
The truth is that they were never really separate from their souls
in the first place, so saying that we "rejoin" our souls is more
metaphorical than literal. I don't want you to mistakenly think
that the spirit and soul are ever separate as they are not. They feel
to us as separate—as humans—but even now, we are connected
to our souls. And when we leave our bodies and return to the
afterlife, we don't technically reunite with our souls; it is more
that we recognize our connection to our higher self, which we
might not have recognized in the physical world. When my soul
chooses to experience a new life—let's say, as Julie—it will create
a new spirit of itself. And that spirit will inhabit a physical human
body that will be Julie. Therefore, when we discuss reincarnation
later in this book, this question will help you understand that
it's not really Bob who is reincarnating; it's Bob's soul, who is
creating a new spirit (a new aspect of itself) that will be known
as Julie. Because Julie shares the same soul as Bob, George, and
Sarah, if she ever experiences a past-life regression, she might
have memories of one of those lifetimes. But to describe it more
accurately, it's her soul's lifetimes that she's experiencing. Because
she is the wave to her ocean (her soul), and they are therefore
connected as one, she is able to recall the other lifetimes of her
soul. The wave doesn't reincarnate as another wave. The ocean

creates a new wave, which is connected both to the ocean and all the other waves that came before it. Why is this important? Well, for example, many people worry that their loved one might reincarnate before they themselves die and return to the afterlife. This "soul versus spirit" explanation helps you understand that their loved one's spirit isn't actually who is reincarnating—it's their loved one's soul that has created a new spirit to experience another lifetime. So, no matter how long a person lives, their loved one will always be there in the spirit world to greet them when they die.

On June 5, Chris visited.

"Hi, Dad; feel me now? I was with you all day yesterday, in the car, on the course and especially at the grave. I felt the intensity of your energy. I know you were hurting but the love was strong and came through. I miss you too. But things were changing in my life on your side. It would have been a very tough time. The happiness I feel now and every day is something I would not have had back there. No regrets on how I got home. I'm here and I feel warm and free. But I miss you very much. I have it both ways. But you don't. You will though when you cross over. I'll be there the moment you step over. The moment you cross you will get it very quickly. You are open to it already. Big advantage, big edge, less of a learning curve. It will be more surprise and less of a learning curve. You will be able to enjoy the time because of this time together. You're learning now. Preparing for the journey, then you will be amazed, not shocked. I was kind of in shock as I zoomed though. Regretting that I did something that resulted in my crossing. You won't have that. You'll see."

"Keep writing. I'm close, real close when you are writing. My spirit is next to you. It's where I choose to be. It's not a favor or an imposition. Think of a subway train, like in Spain. It's clean and

fast and Caroline is guiding you through the tunnels. That is what it will be like for you. And because it's me you will relax, let go and enjoy the ride. Soon, in my time but not that soon. Enjoy the days of your side. Less stress, less bullshit, less fear. I'm always here. It was the ninth hole yesterday was when you stopped hurting. That was because you felt me and I let your soul know that it was okay. Not an ounce less love. Maybe even more because I felt how much love you have for me. My spirit. We are one, dad and I love you. All the things that bring you joy the smell, the warmth, and gentle breezes are around me every day. Constant joy. No sadness or fear. You know it's all good.

Tell everyone I'm still very much around them. Start looking around for the signs I'm there. It's fun to do this for me. They can hear me like you do.

This is our time Dad. Between 3 and 4 a.m. Thanks for loving me all the time. Then and now. It's a wide-open door. Head Chakra, third eye. It's open and I'm here.

I love you too Pop!"
Chris

Well my son isn't afraid to touch on tough subjects. As I've mentioned, Chris dealt with, or didn't deal with, depression. He used pot and alcohol to help him cope. In spite of his substance abuse, he was adored at the frat house and remained a legend back home. Nobody didn't love Chris. He was an amazing friend, and so much fun to be around. But his mom and I worried that if he didn't stumble back to sobriety the world would crumble under his feet. He wasn't going to become a good student and his friends would all move out and graduate (which they have now). I had a plan for him but we ran out of time. However, in my research I came upon the idea of exit points, which I've mentioned. I am convinced that these exit points exist. More than one medium has said that Chris had a number of near-death experiences. Once, he flipped a small pickup truck on a country road and later fell 30 feet down a mine shaft. Why was it the third time, in the canoe, caused him to cross? I don't know. And if he chose the exit point, why has every medium told us that he had an oh fuck moment, when he realized he was leaving earth. Once again, I don't know. Maybe his spirit chose and he wasn't yet aware of it. What I know that is this book is not about finding answers to why. It's all about finding Christopher. And if I find a few answers along the way, that's a bonus.

Chris seems to be very aware that things on this side were about to get rocky, and he sounds relieved to have been able to duck that reality (in true McQuillen fashion). He is very content where he is, which tells me it has to be awesome. Chris was not one to stick around somewhere unless the place was great. He is pushing me to keep getting deeper and do what I'm doing with this book. I'm happy to do it because it keeps me close to my sweet boy.

I need you to understand what it's like to review notes from a year or so ago while writing this book. I am walking back into the conversations between my heartbroken self and my beloved son on the other side. It's amazing that I can go back to a moment when Chris was dictating sentences to me. It's extraordinary to feel that love, that confidence and a contentment that he didn't often feel on this side. It's not unusual for me to go through a visit and think that is absolutely, 100 percent Chris, 100% him. It's also not uncommon to stop writing and begin to wail into a towel hung next to the desk for just those occasions. That he is committed to always being with me on this side until it's my time to cross over is very reassuring. My greatest fear is no longer old age or even death but not feeling him around me. Maybe that's why I'm writing this and why I keep searching. I want to feel him, hear him, smell him and God willing, see him as some mediums do. But I want to make it clear that as rewarding as this journey has been, it's exhausting and often leaves me empty.

On June 9 Chris came through.

"Hi dad; you wanted to know what it's like here. Think of a perfect day. Warm, but not hot. A breeze but never cold. It's like that every day. Every day is the best day and tomorrow will be the best day- office space in reverse. We are all together. One thing. Always trusting always loyal, all close. Love and friendship together. Every being is about love. No motives, no ulterior motives. Just love and joy. Angels full of love and joy, just to let you know they love you. You have them but you can't quite feel them. But you won't let go. Nancine knows, reach out to her about angels. They rock! They are the best. Like Cassidy. Like perfect dogs who love you. They get joy by bringing you joy. It's a great deal. You'll love it."

"It's nice out right? That's why I woke you up. I'm around you now, pop. Feel the back of your neck tingle, that's me. That's how the angels used to let you know they were around you before. Watching you and holding you in the dark times. I love you pop. I know you were hurting yesterday and I took away the sadness. I was comforting you. Gave you my love. Wrapping my arms around you. You are really getting there with being open. I think most people would be surprised. We will do this forever until we are together on the other side. I'll be with you until then, so don't worry about me going away. I can do all of my other world stuff and still ride along with you. It's a bit over your head but you will figure it out. (With my help dad) Stay the course, keep writing the book. People will love it and you will help open eyes. Lots of people don't know what you already know and you are just scratching the surface. Hear those birds...that was

from me. Good morning, pop. I love you Pop, get it. We'll be together but you need to enjoy the run. I'll make sure everything is okay if you let go and… you know the rest pop. It's like playing with monopoly money. I keep proving I'm around to you and will even do more as we both advance. You and me, just like we always liked it. Remember."

"If pine trees with a summer wind blowing through is what you want, then bam it's there.

This is an amazing place. Anything you can imagine. Surfing is something I always wanted to do and you did too, but now I'm doing it. And you're too old. pop. Maybe not. "

"Constant, constantly as the Northern Star (thanks Joni). That's what I am for you. Always forever. It's how it works. All the bullshit to get here and then let go. Like cliff jumping in a warm pool. Let go. You know you are loved so let go."

"Over here if you were shy you still are. I love who I am and wouldn't trade me for any other spirit. I am kind of a star here. Like a big loving perfect frat. I know how proud you are of my leadership. I know that I get that from you. Give my dog a hug for me right now. She sees me come and go all the time."

"I love you Pop. I always loved you. Somehow, I forgot that for a while but now it's back. Like when I was a kid or when I fell down the hole. I took your hand so you would have that memory. Me loving you. Me loving you the most."

Moving on today
Love ya Pop
Chris

This doesn't need a lot of explanation. I do think the *Office Space movie* reference is pretty funny. He also referred to a line in a Joni Mitchell song I am so grateful for the outpouring of love from my boy. If anyone reading has a fear of the other side, then Chris' messages should put you at ease. It sure sounds friggin great to me. Especially since my son is there.

June 24, 2017 Chris visited at 3:19 a.m.

"I remember everything, Pop. Every call, every visit, every talk. It's instant recall here. We were and are very close. Soul Family. But don't worry so much. We will be together again just like before. The airport, road trip to Scottsdale. All of it. I know how much you loved me and wanted the best for me. The clarity on this side is like looking through a window. Like trying to look through a prism.

I loved the shave kit. Tommy B, just like the lighter and the cups I gave you. STAY LIT :)

So proud of that gift. Thanks for bringing the ditty (shave kit). Will is coming out of it. Be patient, I was the same way. He doesn't have alcohol to escape the sadness. Big love, Pop. Be his rock like you were mine. The messenger will show up.

I'm not sad anymore. No guilt about the accident or the hurt. Just pure love for you and my sweet momma. She always had a pure sweet love for me and I couldn't appreciate it. But I do now and let her know that I didn't always get it then. I do now. Don't worry, Pop, we will have all the time in the world together, literally. Enjoy what's left of the world on your side. I'll be there surely, no doubt. Your love matters, always did. Aren't you glad you got up for this?

I've been calling you. I was with you golfing yesterday. Pure swing, pure love, pure everything. It's coming into focus for you Pop. I get it all at once. God, pure love, energy. Stay pure and I'll guide you through it all.

Go out on the deck and look at the sky and know I love you."

Chris

My goodness, this visit was a gift. Chris talked about the drive from Tucson to Scottsdale. On the drive we would take turns playing songs for each other. It was amazing how much we loved the same music and we turned each other on to artists, songs, etc. It was pure fun as we were going from the Ranch in Tucson to a resort in Scottsdale. Our spirits were high and we both loved the company. I wrote about this drive in a song we wrote (Brad Nye and myself) called "Life is honestly so beautiful." He would tell his college pals, "Life is honestly so beautiful, as long as you allow it to be." This Chris McQ saying is embossed on the wrist bands and printed on the posters for the Chris McQ Golf outing. I'm glad those trips were as significant to him as they were to me. That was truly close to heaven on earth for me. He talked about his Tommy Bahama shave kit which was a gift I gave him one Christmas that I knew would be a hit. I brought the kit into my office that morning. I often pick it up and try to smell him on it. He also talked about two gifts he gave me on our last two Christmas' together. For Christmas 2014 he gave me four Tommy Bahama coffee mugs, with four different scenes and each a different color. He really hit the mark with that gift and it made him so proud. Unless I'm traveling I start every day with coffee from one of those mugs. I keep them in a separate cupboard and won't even allow them to be stacked for fear of chipping one. On our last Christmas together, in 2015, he gave me a Tommy Bahama cigar lighter that says "STAY LIT." This was a term I had used for years to indicate being inebriated. As in "boy. was I lit". Well I guess the term came back into vogue, and he thought the gift was sensational. Because it was. Both of those gifts are precious keepsakes that help me feel close to Chris.

He talked about his brother and my need to be patient and supportive. I'll try, Chris. He also talked about the special bond he always had with his momma. She was where he ran to when he was sick, scared or got his heart broken. My God, our heart aches not having him with us in the flesh. It's been two plus years and the reality of it sometimes doesn't fully sink in. By the way, it doesn't get easier. You get a little more used to it, but that's as good as it gets.

All of the mediums I have met with have told me that Chris and I are from the same soul family and Chris refers to this during this meeting.

Here is how Dr. Poonam Bharti KryonIndia, a life coach, describes a soul family:

"Soul family is the spiritual equivalent to your birth family here on Earth. They may take the form of a relative here on Earth, or could be anyone in your life. When you meet them, they feel like your siblings, parents or children. You and your soul family share the same over-soul, so you are all aspects of the same soul."

The reassuring thing for me that knowing we are from the same soul family is knowing we will be reunited again on the other side.

On June 25, our friend Jen Weigel invited us to meet a medium named Sheri Jewel at a wine shop in Evanston. Sally and I brought along our 20-year-old daughter Caroline. Caroline had kept a lot of her grief inside and didn't really buy into our new interest in the other side. As is often the case in these settings I was the only man in the group. We were all sitting on a couch pit and casually chatting when Sheri came in. Jen introduced us and explained how the readings would go. We would meet with Sheri one at a time, in the order in which we arrived, at a table in front of the shop. Sheri was chatting with us when she turned to me and announced, "Well, Christopher is here and I guess you are going now." She headed to the front of the shop and I followed along smiling at the power of my son.

Sheri told me Chris is always near me. He isn't my spirit guide but acts like a guide to me. Chris said he was sorry it happened but he had to go. She told me Chris had been drinking and that he was in a canoe and drowned with three other boys. She told me Chris was showing her a 4ᵗʰ of July when he was a boy. She said he mentioned his dog (who was in the back of my jeep) and my hat (which was a penguin players ball cap in his honor on a chair next to me). He mentioned a shared memory of us skiing, which we did in Beaver Creek together. That was one the best weekends of my life. Sheri told me Chris said I was a good Dad. She said he drank a lot and that I needed to focus and remember. There was nothing that could have been done. It was meant to happen. She did say that Chris does arrange things from the other side.

"Dad you're the best." He acknowledged Mish. Sheri indicated that he showed her a door opening and being in Beaver Creek, Colorado when he was 12. He told Sheri he was with me on the Sarasota beach. He told her that I would start seeing things. He mentioned the band and said "thanks for that." Chris said he was addicted and had a difficult road to recovery. He wanted me to know he was never leaving my side. There is the biggest unbreakable bond between us. He likes the idea of this book, *Christopher's Story*.

He said it was time to heal now. Sheri told me to look into Binaural Beats. (something I did today more than two years later) I have to be honest with you. I didn't realize how good this reading was until I went through my notes. I forgot all about the Beaver Creek reference and so many other accurate and intimate details. I loved that he reinforced my belief that he was next to me, or even walked through me in Sarasota, as Thomas John will tell me in August. I have seen Sheri a few more times and she has become a pal. And Chris seems to have taken to her because when I'm around so is Chris.

On July 3, Chris visited.

"Hi Pop, 18 months, a day, it's all the same. Love is clearer here and I love you. Always did, but now I understand love. Your love, I understand your love now. Your Dad's love from you. I know what pure love feels like and looks like. It's an awakening on new learning. Like speaking French (which I do now). Now I get it. I'm overwhelmed by the love for me. I didn't really feel it on your side. I didn't get it then. But I do now. I know you and mom loved me but it's clear and pure now and I let it flow over me. Thanks for that and I love you both too. I'm full of love. Everything here is love. You can just trust it and accept that's the way it is. Once you get it, there is truly no doubting anymore.

I'll see you at the grave today, because that's what you want to do. I'm with you now; I'm with you in the car. I've strengthened as I know you have. As I get better at it I can show myself to you. In the meantime, it's like showing off. I love my dog. I hear her breathing. When she goes she'll come right to me. She won't be afraid or alone for a moment. You too, Pop. Pat is here, Chingy (a nickname) is here.

I love you dad. Man, you are waking up and opening to my side. Go Bro! We'll get there. This is our time. 3 a. m., thinking and remembering and loving."

I love you
Chris (go with initials)

This message, on a page and a half on legal paper, was intense. It's truly amazing. I am moved by the awakening Chris is feeling and the realization how loved he was and is. He is immersed in a world of pure love and can now understand our love for him. He says he can trust it now. He wasn't a trusting kid on this side, especially of adults. He only trusted a handful of grownups and I was one of the privileged few. There was a time when he was 13 or 14 that I felt he didn't even trust me anymore and that broke my heart. He did come back to me and I always knew that he felt that I would always be there for him.

He talked about being able to show himself to me as we both get better at this. This news made me happier than you could imagine. He then talked about being there when I cross over. Of course, he talked about being there when Cassidy, our dog crosses first. I hope that is due to E.T.A. rather than order of importance. He referred to Pat (Chingy) which was a nickname of some sort for him. Just a snippet to let me know he's there.

On July 12, we were at it again.

"Hi, Dad, I know it's confusing. Don't try to take in too much. You're not that smart. You will get right with it all, you will absorb it. I'm the same, I look the same. I'm your Christopher. With my arm around your neck, loving my Dad. Don't worry. It's soft and warm. Even the rain is a soft warm rain. It feels awesome. It's never cold. Keep reaching, keep meditating, keep getting outside of your head and body. I'm here to guide you.

Remember. I remember every moment. Every hug, every kiss, hand in hand walking on the sidewalk in Naples, to laying in a hospital bed in Scottsdale. I remember it all with a blink. Total loving recall. I'm around you always. I can do that. We won't lose this ever.

Trust it (God) trust me, Chris.

Love the tattoo. You didn't have to put it on your arm. I know you love me with all of your heart and soul. But it's you, Pops, that's for sure. We get a kick out of you. I get a kick out of you and you make me proud. My dad is trying so hard. I love you. Glad you're here. I'm always here when you call at 3 -4 a.m. Our time, pops. Always will be. You've got plenty of time over there but you will never be without me by your side. There and here, stop worrying and breathe deep.

Love the outing. Love your friends. Love our friends. They will all come through. Not just for me but for you too, pal. I never left you even when you thought I did. Even when I pulled back, you were my rock, my real. You still are. Just write it and don't think about it.

I'm with you when you write songs. Hi Brad, did you get my feather? I know. Love the pictures…. my guy. You'll play today just wait and see.

Will is coming around. It will be fine, just love him. Don't hold back anything. Time means nothing here so don't get hung up on it. Feel me around you pops? It's where I like to be. You aren't pulling me away from anything. Write that book, Pop. It will matter."

Gotta go. Walking the beach in moonlight, thinking of you and momma.

Love you
Chris

Most of what is communicated here doesn't need too much clarification. Even though on the previous visit he told me to go with the initials, I had gotten a tattoo on my right arm, above my palm tree tattoo, of a feather with Christopher's name spelled out under it. But he said he loved it so all good. He seems to send Brad Nye feathers ever since we wrote the "I'll send you Feathers" together and Brad will send me an occasional iPhone pic of one. He must like Brad because he referred to him as "my guy." Brad actually sent the song to Julian Lennon, who he knows, because Julian said in an interview that his dad told him that when he died he would send him feathers. We will see what happens. But six degrees of Kevin Costner right. (Both Chris and I always felt *Bull Durham* was his best movie.) And, he finished with telling me to just love his brother Will, unconditionally. Even though like his older brother he can be a complete pain in the ass.

Hopefully by now you've discarded any thoughts of this being my way of processing my grief, even though it is. This is a dialogue with my adored son who has crossed over. I know it. There is so much evidence of that fact. One of the most solidifying for me is that there are moments that I read what Chris has told me and know for a fact I would never say that. "You were my rock, my real. You still are." He even knows I am hesitating writing it down and he chided me by saying, "Just write it down." When he says, "We get a kick out of you," I'm looking through my notes and wondering, who is we? He mentions his friend Pat is with him, but I'm not sure if that's who Chris is talking about. I didn't create these thoughts or I would know more. And boy, do I want to know more.

On Thursday July 27, I had a session with Andrew Anderson. On this afternoon, as usual, we adjourned to his office. As with most, if not all, visits with Andrew, he comments that Chris is in the room and traveled with me, as usual. Chris told Andrew we were going on a trip. He said Chris would be with us in Canada. He said Chris was holding balloons which signified a birthday. He told Andrew that not much has changed with Will, and he was worried about him. He wants him to try more.

Chris told Andrew he was proud of me and that I was getting stronger. He's happy that Sally and I seem to be working things out despite the grief. With so much going on Chris said he was having a hard time keeping up. Andrew said, "He's coming to Canada," and he's been spending a good deal of time with Sally.

Chris said that he is with Patrick, one of the boys who drowned with him. He mentioned a Baptism.

Chris told Andrew that he is so happy right now. He's happy about the book and wants to be on the cover. He's proud of the new song. Andrew said he is and will always be handsome, so good looking.

He wanted to talk about Caroline. Chris said he sent her a bird in Spain and sends her birds in Milwaukee. He said she is missing signs and that he pulls her hair. He's tugged on it to let her know it's him. He's proud of her and will send her butter-flies. He loves his music. He said that he will come to her in a dream (which she acknowledged to me right after this reading that he has).

I asked a few questions and Chris told me we will walk through the next life like we walked through this one. He told Andrew that this will be Aunt Marcia's last Crystal Beach and we should relish it (God I hope he miscalculated). And that the last day of the upcoming golf outing will be perfect. "Another day in paradise."

Andrew asked me if I had just returned from eye doctor, which I had. Chris said he was with me. He said he just wanted to show it's really him, which is the most important thing to him.

The experience of getting a reading from a really good medium is s very spiritually lifting. In my case it's validating as all of the messages I'm getting are consistent with the messages received from the professionals.

Chris talked a lot about Canada. The annual McQuillen family reunion. The birthday he referenced was his godmother

Marcia's, who he adored and vice versa. When I talked earlier
about Chris only trusting a handful of adults. Aunt Marcia was
one of the chosen few. We celebrated her birthday on this trip.
Another side note is that the previous Christmas I had booked
a phone reading for Marcia with Andrew Anderson. While in
Canada we made the call and Andrew did a reading for her.
Because I booked the slot and Andrew was my medium I just
assumed that the reading would be about Christopher. However,
spirits have their own agenda.

Although Chris did come through to Marcia and expressed
his love, the majority of the reading was her recently deceased
husband Tom coming through. Although Marcia told me in
detail about the reading, it's her private reading and not for me
to share. Tom did tell her many things about their life together
that only he would know. And he thanked her for giving him such
a full and loving life. A second chance (both had been married
before. He also made amends for some issues at the end. This
allowed Marcia to embrace his loving memory and spirit and
forgive him the late inning missteps. With Marcia giving me so
much throughout my life I was very happy to give her a gift that
touched her soul.

Chris mentioned his pal Pat again which made me smile
because we loved Pat. Chris mentioned a baptism I didn't know
if it was this side or something on his side. Even now I'm not
sure what he meant.

Maybe it's time to talk about the clairs. As I mentioned each
medium uses one or more of the clairs to connect to spirit.

When I communicate with Chris it is through clairaudience
and clairsentience. I'm getting better at it. But I would love
nothing more than to be able to see Chris, as the clairvoyants do.

On August 6, Chris visited. We just returned from Canada
and I couldn't find my AKL sweatshirt which had been put

together in his honor in 2016. All Founder's Day sweatshirts had to be approved and sanctioned before being distributed. Mine was neither. I am so proud of that. I love these boys. I searched the house and even emailed the rental agent. She promised to check the house, but I was heartbroken.

"Let it go dad. It's a sweatshirt, it's not me. I was with you all week. I was with you at each gathering. I was still there when you went home early. They all loved me and I loved them."

Just to clarify my siblings, their kids and in many cases, their kids gather every year in Crystal Beach, Ontario for a McQ family reunion. My Christopher loved being a McQuillen and was adored by the family. "I was special to them and that's love. I still am. I will come to Bridget (his cousin) and heal her. Kerry's is working with both girls from here. She is always there, all the time. They need to open up and see her. "

"Wow, you really are letting it go. That's big progress. Hold onto nothing. It's all given to you when you come home, when you cross. Like going to Wegmans on the way to Crystal Beach. It's all handed to you and everything else is left behind except the love. I love you. I have a pure love for you. Very clear. I've been here to talk with you. But you have to let go of the doubts that's it's me. It's always you and me. I'm still here. My arm is around you like at the Saints game (see cover). Funny, right. Back on a beach again, in the moonlight walking on the sand. That's us. Walk your path Pops —then come to me and join me here.

Resent no one. Be love, be accepting. Work at it. I can't even remember drowning, Pop. Let that go. It's so wonderful that I would choose that path to get here. You'll get it. I'll be here for you. Keep trying-keep pushing- keep writing. I like the new chair. I'll be with you tomorrow. I'll always be with you. Don't fear that. It's forever, that's a guarantee. I'm with you Pop. Don't over think it. I still

look like me. It's me. Thanks for getting up. We both needed this.
Lots of emotion in Canada. Lots of energy, lots of love.
Nothing stays the same- but love. "

"Heading back, love you Dad."
Chris

This one was really moving. The good news is that later on that
same morning I found my sweatshirt, which coincidentally I'm
wearing right now. And, no I don't wear the AKL sweatshirt
every time I write, not every time. I do think I had to be willing
to let it go, before it was sent back to me.

He really does crack me up even from the other side. Wegmans
is a northeast grocery chain that has everything. Meats, beers,
produce, etc. It even has a Buffalo sports team shop. I usually
pick up a new Bills baseball cap along with a week's worth of
groceries for Canada. This year I picked up a Buffalo Bills cloth
folding chair. This was to replace the maple leaf folding chair
that finally collapsed. I keep this chair in the back of my jeep
along with a bag of cleaning supplies and scissors which I use
to keep the gravestone pristine. I love that Chris likes my new
chair. He gets me. He talked about loving and being loved by the
McQuillens. He did and they do. He was discreetly busting my
chops for leaving the family events early. He never left early and
apparently still doesn't. This brought a memory and a smile to
my face. When he was about three-years-old we were attending
the wedding of Sally's step brother Steve on Cape Cod. We were
renting a cottage and a local gal was babysitting my kids. I left the
wedding a few hours in and strolled back to check on the kids.
I hate parties and at one point in every evening I always stroll
off. I checked in at the cottage and my Caroline was sleeping
soundly. But Chris was wide awake in the pack and play. There

was a party going on and he knew it, and that just wouldn't do. I walked in and he began to jump up and down smiling and calling out to me. As a responsible parent I knew what had to be done. I swooped him in my arms threw him on my shoulders and marched back to the party only now feeling whole. We arrived, and danced the night away, sometimes with him on my shoulders and sometimes with just him in the middle of a loving crowd.

By the way, these are just the moments when I have to stop and let the tears flow. I feel sorry for myself for a moment, and then thank God for giving me Chris in the first place. Well anyway back to my point, from a very early age, my son never left a celebration early.

He mentioned, "My arm around you like at the Saints game."

When he was in St. Paul after a stint at the Retreat, I came up to visit him and bring him up his beloved Jeep Wrangler (with a Buffalo Bills tire cover), and a new cell phone. He showed me St. Paul and we visited the Cathedral where he would meditate in the morning. We shopped for clothes for him, ate great meals, golfed and went to a St. Paul Saints minor league baseball game. We had a ball. He bought a Saints Ball cap and we sat in the sun enjoying each other and the minor league atmosphere. There are a number of pictures I cherish from that weekend. But the one I love most is hanging on my office wall. There are two pictures actually. One at that Saints game with Chris' right arm around my shoulder, and another when I was holding him when he was about 2 ½ years old.

My God, I miss that boy.

The next thing he talked about is very affirming that it's him talking to me and not my mind placating my broken heart. He said, "I don't even remember drowning Pop. Let that go. It's wonderful that I would choose that path to get here." There is no way on earth that I would use the term wonderful to describe the incident that caused him to cross. Then he goes on to tell me, "You'll get it, I'll be here for you."

He finishes by telling me that nothing stays the same but love. Thanks Chris, I love you so.

On August 13, 2017 Sally and I had a private reading in person with Thomas John. We chose to split it up in two thirty-minute individual sessions because that's kind of how we do things. It works for us.

I was a little cautious because I didn't want to get my hopes up and be disappointed. Thomas John is a nationally known medium. But also remember that in a small group reading I came away disappointed. That is until I re listened to the reading while documenting it for this book. I had somehow missed how impactful it was. Maybe because most of the messages were for Sally, and not for me. I should be a spiritually bigger man…I'm not. Also remember that we experienced Thomas at the Wilmette theatre on Dec 13, 2016.

He knocked us out with his ability to connect with Chris, and his descriptions and messages were absolutely spot-on. I wasn't really sure what to expect.

We met at a conference room at. The Allerton Hotel. Sally went first and truthfully, I was happy she went first because my stomach was in my throat and I needed to calm down. When attending a reading I always carry a leather zipper folder with outer pockets. I pack it with pictures, a legal pad and some stones, and a few mementos, which I rotate. Sometimes I bring Chris' license, which has been absconded by William. (you figure it out) I sometimes bring his AKL frat pin or his St. Christopher medal from his baptism. I have numerous times brought his Buffalo Bills #13 Jersey that he wore so often it practically wore out. The boys at AKL presented me with a McQuillen #13 jersey framed and signed by each brother. It hangs on the wall just above my computer screen. It makes me smile (and sometimes cry.) This day I brought his Bills jersey, a few stones, and his St. Christopher medal that was given him by his adoring godfather Michael. As Sally walked into the conference room I began to relax, as much as I can relax, that is. I began to talk to Chris and repeated my earlier invite to come through. I also let him know how much I loved him. But seeing as I was sitting in a hotel hallway in downtown Chicago, with a briefcase full of pictures and personal objects from his past after fronting a hefty fee, I think he knew that.

Thomas is amazing and allows you to record your sessions. The recording is necessary because the messages come pretty quickly and you don't want to miss a message from your son because you are writing down the last message. My process is to keep the recording, listen to it occasionally and when it's time to report on that reading, I transcribe the session on a legal pad before entering it into my book. Since readings are very personal, when I'm writing about other people's readings, including Sally's, I write about validating points but I don't write in detail because those messages are between the spirit and the recipient. Before I write about anything in someone's reading I clear it with the one receiving messages. So here we go….

I'm going to write about Sally's reading first even though I didn't hear it until the ride home. Thomas asks Sally how she wants it to go. "Ask specific questions of spirit or just what comes." Sally asked if they could just go with what comes and ask a few questions at the end. I did mine the same way.

"Couple of things coming through," said Thomas. "Someone from your mom's side named Sarah is coming through. She was maybe 100. She's helping you. I'm also getting someone, a younger guy. I wrote down 21. There is also a girl on your spouse's side. Something to do with her brain. Your dad is coming through. He had a narcissistic energy. Because you were creative there was a disconnect." He then talked about our daughter Caroline and her traveling. "It's how she's coping."

Thomas then began to talk about the event that caused Chris to cross over. "It's very cold weather. He previously had a number of very close calls. He was very loving." "Were there other people who died with your son? I see them around him." Did this happen around Christmas?" "I feel Peru." Chris went on to tell Thomas that we gave him a very happy life, we kind of spoiled him. He wants his mom to focus on her book, and not leave anything out for his sake. He offered an apology to his sister for not being a better brother on our side. He said there were lots of people at his funeral. Chris said that there is "so much he's learning on the other side" and Thomas said he was a very old soul.

This was amazing and truthfully, I only wrote down about half of what Chris, Thomas, and Sally discussed. But he truly is gifted. Just opening up with Sally's adored grandmother connecting was a precious gift to Sally. Sally was named after her grandmother who was called Nanny by all the grandchildren and great grandchildren. (Sally is a nickname for Sarah.) She was an amazing woman who lived to 100. She attended Smith College at a time when most women weren't even completing high school. She was warm, strong, sweet and wise. Sally and Nanny had a very close relationship and Sally would visit her quite often, especially toward the end of her life when her husband (Bompa) crossed. I was wondering when Nanny would come through for Sally. Then I thought of course Nanny came through when it was appropriate. That's Nanny.

Thomas mentioned a 21-year-old male, which of course is Chris. He was 21 when he crossed over and I think he always presents himself at that age.

What is truly amazing, and I mean amazing, is the amount of information Thomas brings forward almost immediately. When he spoke, he connected with four spirits absolutely connected to Sally. First her beloved Nanny, her namesake; Next Chris. He then touched on my niece, Kerry. Although she was as mentioned from my side of the family, she was so very close to Sally. And then her father Warren, whom Thomas has connected with before. He describes his personality traits with the accuracy of a psychic sharp shooter.

Thomas said Chris wants her to "focus on her book." She is in the midst of writing one about raising, loving and losing a challenging son.

Come on, if you aren't completely on board now then there is no hope for you.

By the way, if you are still with me…buckle up. I am about to tell you about a most amazing half hour. Sally walked out of the conference room and we locked eyes and hearts. I knew she just spent time with our precious Christopher. And it was my turn. As I told you before that for a myriad of reasons I have a veritable flock of butterflies in my stomach before any session. I am anxious, scared (not because of reaching spirit, but rather that there is a weak or no connection), and very excited. Think about this. What would you give to have a half hour to spend with someone precious whom you've lost? Now imagine that person is your child. Okay, you get it now, right?

Thomas began with the same question he asked Sally regarding the reading about how I wanted to do it. I said I would like to let it flow and then ask a few questions toward the end.

"Hopefully," I said," it's with my boy."

"Did he smoke or did he drink?" asked Thomas. I replied that he smoked pot and did drink, a lot. Thomas told me, "when I tap into his energy that he's really, really advancing on the other side." Thomas told me, "He was talking about you going to his grave and sitting there. You'll sit there and talk to him and you'll go to his grave a lot." Thomas said that often when spirits bring that up, they will say, "I'm not there anymore." Chris is saying that he "likes that time with you and him." He feels close to you and you and him really connect there.

Watching Thomas work is truly astounding. When connecting with a spirit, he squints and leans forward when he's really trying to focus. He is literally answering to a different dimension and he taps into the other side. "When we're eavesdropping, I hear his "huh," "yeah,' and "okay." It's incredible. I have to restrain myself from blurting out, "what did he say?"

But I don't, because I know Thomas will tell me and I don't want to break the connection they have.

Thomas continued channeling Chris. "I have no idea why, but I just saw Marv Levy…why am I seeing him?" I had to laugh and explain the McQuillen connection, sometimes bordering on obsession with the Buffalo Bills. Chris, as I have mentioned before, was a huge Bills Fan. This seemed to confuse Thomas while making me smile. I am writing what Thomas says as he connects. Sometimes he stops in midsentence and picks up somewhere else. But that's how he does it so that how I'm writing this.

I can tell Thomas is now listening to Chris. "He's saying that everything is happening according to a divine timing- even though it's painful. You definitely will see him again, you will talk to him again, and connect again in a reality where you are together.

He then looks over my shoulder and says "There is somebody coming through that left two kids, two boys. She died in her forties in 2012 or 2013 her name is Kerry." The fact that my niece Kerry came through was a very pleasant surprise, even though I've been told that that Kerry was there to help Christopher cross over. A loving pay back for Chris staying on to temporarily nanny her two boys when she passed of an aneurism in Feb 2013. I adored my niece and it was such a wonderful surprise to have her come through.

Thomas explains that lots of people have jobs on the other side. "Your son is like the pied piper for kids. He really likes to work with children on the other side. Kids that have crossed over, you know spirits that passed young. Spirits can have regrets, things they wish were different and he said he would have liked to have had his own family. And that's hard for him. But he knows there are other things he has to work on. But he would have loved to have been a Dad. He would have been a great Dad."

Thomas asked, "Did he have friends who died?" I explained that three boys drowned with him. "Okay, because he is saying he is with his friends. We're all doing different things over here. "

Thomas told me that I have a living son who's struggling with this all and that Chris is "trying to help and visit him but I can't really connect."

Thomas asked if I went to my son's grave recently. I answered that I was there the day before. "He hears your prayers, which are your thoughts." Thomas asked me if Chris ever had a near death experience. He had two, I responded. "One thing he's saying is that he did not realize, until he got to the other side the finality of life. It didn't fully click with him. There was a recklessness and feeling of invincibility. I can feel your son was very loving and very stubborn."

Thomas asked about his drinking and asked if it contributed to his crossing over. He's saying he's free of that. He doesn't struggle in that way anymore.

Chris told Thomas that he wishes he "spent more time with his sister. He wishes that he had that a little more, a little more time with her."

Thomas said he was seeing baseball and steaks and asked about it. Chris and I attended many baseball games together, from spring training to World Series games and the time together watching games was important. A picture of him standing at the dugout is now my screensaver. But I only posted that a few days ago. I truly believe there is synchronicity at play here

Webster's World Diction defines synchronicity as: *"the simultaneous occurrence of events that appear significantly related but have no discernible causal connection."* This mention of baseball did not at first sink in. And I actually only added it when going through this reading for a casual edit. Trust me people, these aren't unconnected events that's I'm pasting together to make a collage to soothe my grief. These connect. These are real. Baseball played a part in our lives, and I almost missed it. I tried to. But Chris wouldn't let me. As for steaks, we loved steak dinners together. Any weekend together always included a steak dinner at a high-end steak house or a local joint. One of my favorite dinners together was in Scottsdale in the fall of 2010. I picked Chris up at the Ranch for the weekend and we drove up to Scottsdale. We passed a sign for Fogo de Chao, the Brazilian Steakhouse, and that was that. We went that night and, watching Chris dig in was pure joy for me; after all, he had had three months of ranch food. We ate like we were going to the electric chair and then returned to the hotel to chainwatch pay per view movies. This memory ranks as truly one of my all-time favorites, but like *baseball*, I only wrote about it while editing the words from my visit with Thomas.

Thomas said Chris was talking about a necklace of his that I have. I opened my closed left hand to reveal my son's St. Christopher medal that he received at his baptism from his godfather.

Chris told Thomas that I am in his room a lot. That is of course true; his room is my office where I am sitting writing this book. It's also where I meditate and hear from Chris for our early morning rendezvous. I feel him here, and I smell him here.

Chris told Thomas that Caroline will continue to travel (she is on her way to Peru next month). Thomas thinks that Chris may try to connect with her when she travels. I am hoping that she feels him in Machu Picchu. Chris visited there and considered it a sacred place. Below is a photo of my sweet boy overlooking Machu Picchu in 2012 & Caroline in 2018.

Machu Picchu 2012

Machu Picchu 2018

Thomas asked me, "Is there a Bud and Mary? Were they close? Did they live far away? Was there a geographical distance?" Bud and Mary are Chris' maternal grandparents. My parents had crossed before any of my kids were born. Bud and Mary loved him very much and there was a geographic distance because they moved to the North Woods near Eagle River Wisconsin in 1999.

Just more validation....

Thomas said that I also have a lot of psychic abilities and would start feeling and sensing things from Chris. He will continue to move things around in my office as confirmation that he is doing that and because he thinks it's funny.

Chris said that we did enough for him. "His death was his vibration." Thomas told me that he is expanding over there and is a seeker of knowledge. Chris said that although we both loved him a tremendous amount that it's easier to connect with me than his mom from the spirit world. There is more of a fluid connection between us but as his mom works on reaching him, the connection will expand for her as well.

Thomas asked if anyone had returned from a big trip in the last few weeks. I explained that Caroline had returned from Spain. He said Chris was with her, even though she is a bit closed off. Caroline did mention to me that Chris came to her in a dream at the end of her trip in Majorca.

Thomas asked if I have any letters from Chris. This gave me the opportunity to ask about my channel writing. I produced a recent communication from Chris. Thomas took a moment and said, "That's him. Spirit will communicate in any form they feel. And yeah, that's him. He actually wants you to put it all in a book. Chris said you are going to help a lot of men who suffer. Because it's a different energy, it's easier for women to embrace this sort of thing. He wants you to be a spokesperson for that. He's going to keep coming to you with that stuff and you just keep saving it. The writing is definitely him… I don't know why he connects with you that way. I guess he just feels like you listen and you're getting it, so he's just doing it."

Thomas asked whether I had any other questions.

I asked about Sarasota, where I had felt so close to Christopher on the beach at night.

Thomas asked me if we were planning to buy a house there. He said that Chris likes the energy there for you. It doesn't have to be tomorrow but he thinks that you should think about buying there. There is some sort of vibration that is very, very positive there.

Back to the question on the beach;" Yeah that was him. Things just have to align. If you're open, with the right environment and they're ready …. It almost feels in a weird way that I'm getting that he kind of went through your body, almost like he went through you."

Then I asked Thomas about writing the song, "I'll Send You Feathers." "Yeah, that was him."

And then the toughest question. I asked whether, when he crossed were there others there to greet him and whether that was grueling.

"There were people there to greet him. Because the boys all went over together they had all the love from all the loved ones. There were a lot of people there. He didn't feel alone. More of a feeling of confusion. He didn't really know what was going on. He was kind of out of it. I will be honest with you that he's telling me that for a few moments, a few seconds, it was kind of scary. I feel like it was over quite quickly."

Circling back to the channel writing Thomas said that "One of the reasons you know the words are from spirit is that something will come to you and you say to yourself, 'that's weird I haven't thought about that in a long time.' That's kind of how you know."

I thanked Thomas and we said goodbye. I needed to push myself up and out of the chair, because I didn't want to leave. He had brought Christopher through so vividly that I didn't want to break the connection. But it was temporarily broken and it was time to go.

I don't think I need to clarify anything about this reading. It was validating rejuvenation of the soul. But as I read it now, it's also heartbreaking. I need a minute to compose myself as I finish.

Although I somehow almost missed it, Thomas drew me back to baseball being a connection with Chris. Like Jimmy Buffett's music, baseball was a sort of glue for us.

Baseball absolutely played a part in both of our lives. I've been to a few games including a couple of Cubs games since he crossed… and I know he's there with me.

One quick note. Yesterday was Chris' 24th birthday. His college friends, most of whom have graduated, organized the Second Chris McQuillen pub crawl the night on Saturday, April 14, 2018. While getting ready to attend I was showering and singing the song we wrote together and I was crying. When I walked out of the bathroom I looked down and at my feet was a small white feather. It probably came from a pillow or comforter, but I will tell you I've never seen one there before. I thanked Chris remembering what his friends have always said, "Chris would never let you not have a good time."

We attended the event which was so wonderful. Sixty plus friends gathered in celebration of the friend they love so much. Chris' spirit was everywhere in that room.

On August 19, 2017 Chris and I had another 3 a.m. visit.

"Hi Dad, you are wide awake this morning. Thomas brought you close. Don't stress; it's all really fine. All of it. The outing, the work

and Will. He's opening up now if you keep it open. Walk across the bridge and let him trust you. Bail him out and be his support, like you were mine. I always knew you would take care of it, even though I was always afraid to come to you. I hated admitting that I needed you. I didn't know until I got here that you needed me too. Kind of sweet really. I'm here…back of the neck Pop, that's me. Thomas John nailed it; he really did. I was right there with both of you guys. Sarasota Pop, it was sweet walking right with you. Don't freak out. I'm not going anywhere. It's not a crowded bus terminal. I'll find you and we will be together like on your side. Give Raul a hug for me. He was family to me and I belonged. I loved that (bed)room and those people. Even the stale beer smell made me feel at home. I do miss that. I don't miss the cold though. It's not ever cold here. Warm and soft blue breezes. You will get it. Just accept for now and know I love you and miss you (despite what mediums say), I do. Yep it's me your boy. I'm a good boy? Remember it made you laugh. I loved that. I remember graduation and golfing. Everything Pop. You really tried and I love that now. Keep reaching out and we can get better at this. Even closer. Thank your boys for coming through with the outing. My kind of guys. Did you get my message to write the book? Get it going, it will be great. Edit this and go to bed.

I'll see you at the grave today, Pop"
Love you
Chris

This doesn't need much explanation. The crowded bus terminal reference makes me smile. It confirms that this isn't me. It's a great visual but I certainly didn't originate it. But I also love that it means when I cross I won't be lost in a crowd. He'll be right there. I'm in the final stages of organizing his Second Annual

Chris McQ Golf Outing which will take place on Sept 11, and as usual my friends have come through. It's so nice of him to acknowledge them. It's rewarding to read about the love he felt for his friends in DeKalb and that the frat house was a home for him, complete with the smell of stale beer. It's even more heart-warming because I just spent an evening with all his college pals a few days ago. He referred to "I'm a good boy… 'That was his response whenever I would comment *good boy* about something. He would make a funny face and respond in a juvenile voice, "I'm a good boy?" and I would crack up. As far as warm and soft blue breezes??? Well, he promises me I'll get it. Just not on this side, I think.

On September 1, Chris visited.

"Hi Dad, where ya been? Busy with the plans for my golf outing? Focus on my friends. They all still love and remember. I'm around them they; just don't know it. But they are in the process of believing. It will come. I've been with you a lot this week. I love when we golf together. I'm there, don't doubt it. When I told you before that we would be together, I meant we're really together. Thomas John made that crystal clear to you. I always felt safe with you and that's how I feel all the time over here. Safe and peaceful and warm and loved. Not too bad Pops."

What you are doing with Allen is great. We are right next-door Pop. Energy surrounding you, loving you, warming you, keeping you safe (sometimes). And sometimes we push too far like I did. But I'm happy, really good. I love you, Pop. Keep feeling me. It's impressive how much your love comes through. My friends here can tell how much you love me like my friends on your side could always tell. You're a good guy, Pop. I learned a lot about love from you. Your friends are all rallying. We both have good friends. Hi,

Uncle Mike. Man, you're wide open and dialed in this morning. I just sent you SARASOTA so you know. I love what you are doing for Allen. It will help him open the door. It will all come flooding in. You'll see. No bullshit Pop. Mike Crane says thanks. He's good here. He misses his boys though. I'm a regular fucking chatty Kathy this morning. I'm around you and you are so dialed in with the outing that I feel you so close. You keep going and I'll take care of the other stuff. Keep writing, it will help dads who feel helpless. Keep it up."

"Yeah, dad I was nine. I loved that day. You and me just the way I like it. Thanks for always opening up and loving me. I'll send you something during the outing. Look for it."

I truly love you Pop. Always and forever.
Chris

What a wonderful visit. By now we were days away from the Second annual Chris McQ Golf outing to benefit Penguin Players & In Balance Ranch. These were two amazingly worthy causes that Chris had been involved in and spiritually benefitted from. Being involved in the organization process was comforting and made me feel especially close to my son. I loved working on every aspect from menu planning to games to fundraising to securing donations for silent auction items to pairings. I want to make something very clear to you. As a car dealer I had attended scores of golf outings and I hated them. They were a business obligation and I treated them as such. There were a few exceptions that I really enjoyed but they were few and far between. I did however learn from these outings and implemented their best practices.

Chris' outing is by far the best run and most enjoyable event I have ever attended and I suspect for everyone involved from players, to donors to employees to volunteers. It's a wonderful day of golf, celebration, fellowship, food, libation and music. It is always held on the second Monday in September. The proof of its success is that I could easily double the number of participants with a second email. But that would put a damper on an event that flows so well as it is. Let me tell you a secret. Although it's a fundraiser, the reason for the event is to celebrate my son. Pure and simple. My friends, his friends, and our families all together to spend a day full of laughter and love in his name. The fact that we are able to donate money to two great causes is the icing on the cake for me. My pals all put together activities at their clubs and homes to extend the joy over four wonderful days. They donate their time, money, musical gifts, lots of chocolate, and their support. Think of it as a Woodstock but with attendees fully clothed, gourmet food, and the venue is high end golf club, not a muddy field. So, don't think of it as Woodstock. The one and only downside to the event is the emptiness I feel when it's over. I actively plan this event for months, and I am giddy with anticipation for weeks before. I have friends and family coming in from Virginia, Florida, and Arizona. The house is filled with caps, wristbands and silent auction items. I have various clip boards with events and envelopes full of checks. My office looks more like shipping and receiving than a home office. I wake up early to work on the event before I start my business day, and I work on it again in the evening. There is a natural letdown after any big event and after this one, it is a really big letdown. When the house is back to empty and the cardboard boxes are relegated to the basement I feel a temporary emptiness. Or rather I feel the return of the emptiness, after a brief respite. The week after I am deluged with compliments and comments on the work load and how well everything went. I smile and accept the compliments, but only the closest to me know the truth. It's spiritual oxygen, I need this to breathe. This event, like this book, brings me closer to Chris than air. I hope you get it.

He referred to being nine, as I was writing about us playing at Wrigley, I couldn't figure out how old he was. I think that this is what he was referring to. I think. But I thought he might have been 10; I'm just not sure.

Chris said that he loved what I was doing for Allen which I should explain. As I mentioned earlier Al Conrad is my oldest and one of my closest friends (actually we have always used the word *pals* since high school.) We have been through thick and thin together despite the years and miles between us. I found God through sobriety and Allen found him through loss. Although we both said the Prayer of St. Francis every morning for three years in high school, the words only came to life after spiritual awakenings experienced by each of us. On March 31, 2005, Allen's wife, Debbie, lost her battle with cancer. They were soulmates for sure. I had the opportunity to visit with her a few days prior to her death as we were down in Naples for spring break. She knew it was near the end and I promised her I would look after Allen. But as usual, he ended up looking after me more. When Christopher crossed in January 2016, Allen came to Chicago for Chris' wake and funeral, and both subsequent golf outings. He attended the most recent outing in spite of Hurricane Irma. What's the difference between evacuating an area earmarked for natural disaster and flying out to attend a golf outing for Christopher? No difference to Allen Conrad. Allen had plans in place for months so the trick was getting his new wife Sandy out before the storm. It took all three of us on computers and Chris moving things around to get Sandy out of Sarasota and on her way to Chicago on Friday, the day before the hurricane.

I was not at all surprised when I picked Allen up at the airport on Friday morning. If I had to choose who I would bet on to come through, Al Conrad or a hurricane named Irma, my money's on Conrad every time.

The plan was for me to pick up Al at O'Hare and we would drive straight to Milwaukee Country Club to join my close buddies Mike Holmberg and Rick Blommer for our first round of golf. Rick grew up in Milwaukee and he's been a member there all his life. We would play a round, grab a bite and then I would surprise Al with a visit to Andrew Anderson, my medium pal, a mere 91 miles away. The reason that this had to be a complete surprise is that I really wanted to do something special for my pal but he is both humble and proud and I needed to ambush him to make it work.

Unfortunately, I had to let the cat out of the bag when, after ordering dinner at the club and waiting 45 minutes, there was no sign of our food. I had to tell him why we had to leave. He was excited, nervous and grateful all at once, and no doubt a little hungry.

He had had plenty of family on the other side to contact -- his mom and Dad who I knew and loved and of course, Debbie. I loved that Chris mentioned and approved of this gesture of love for my pal. But that visit is still a few days away....

Chris then told me that Mike Crane says *thanks*. I loved that. Mike is Jimmy Crane's father who crossed over in July 2009. Jimmy joined us in Canada the month after his Dad's passing for the annual McQuillen A.D.D. fest and was immediately accepted as one of us. Like my boy, Jimmy was wild and prone to find trouble. But he was such a sweet boy and he loved my Chris. Up to that time neither one of them could have made a single good decision if they had a gun to their head. Jimmy and Chris remained close and Jimmy is still part of our family. Jimmy has been in recovery for three years and is an agent in the Los Angeles area. Chris and Jimmy's dad always liked each other and Chris was invited on a number of Crane family adventures involving private jets and resorts in exotic places. Remember, "Dad it's a better deal." Well it turns out that Mike Crane's headstone is about 20 paces from Chris' and that's comforting to me. Occasionally when visiting Chris, I will head over and shine up Mike's stone. I also put a chip on Mike's grave acknowledging Jimmy's anniversary. That's why Mike is saying thanks. It is so reassuring and comforting to hear that he's really good on the other side. And, that he misses his boys though. I know the feeling Mike.

On Thursday September 7, the day before the first leg of the Chris McQ Memorial Golf weekend, Chris visited.

"Hi Dad, it's me. Feel me on the back of your neck. You know by now. Looking forward to the weekend. Always me, that's so cool. Back of the neck is my way. It's actually the spirits way. Al is trying and I will help. I know it's important to you. You can ask me for help you know. Go ahead, I will do what I can just like you always did. Always. I know that now. Pure love for you and for mom, for Will and Caroline. No resentments or feeling edgy or pressure, just love. They loved and love me so much, I know what it is now. I couldn't know it then though, couldn't know. "

"The printer, that's me. The feeling on the back of your neck and warm up your spine. That's a new one, but it's undoubtedly me. Open up Pop and get this book going after the outing. One hundred pages that's from me. Clear your mind and heart of money or any pressure and be pure this weekend. I'll golf with you and will guide your shot, your hand. It's me. Clear and pure Pops. Love my friends, I do. I watch over them. It's funny really. So young and such pure love. I knew their hearts even then. Grateful to them. They made my world loved. Not that you didn't but it was acceptance. Hard to do at home. But I love you and love

visiting at the grave. Love my dog. You and mom are connecting. It's about time. I've been working my ass to get that flow going. Keep it up. Pull your weight Pop, you have enough of it. Get it. You're not cold anymore Pop. Nice shirt. I love those sweatshirts. Tell them that. You've got it all going Pop, sage-candles. The sage reminds you of my smell. That sweet-sweat smell. I know it and miss that. It keeps me forever in front of your mind. Walking into a room and smelling me. That's sweet Pop, I miss you too. "

"I'll always be here connected to you, and I'll walk you over when it's time. But it's not. So, this is it. Better than most though. We get it... you get it."

"Go eat and look at the moon. I'm looking at you and smiling. Feels the hugs Pop, feel it, Dad."

Love
Chris

Can I just say that my Chris is friggin amazing! I do know when he's around by the tingle on the back of my neck. And boy was he around for this visit. He told me he would help with Al and what that meant was Allen was struggling to get out of Sarasota for the event with the incoming hurricane and all that entails. He had to arrange for Sandy's travel and secure his two homes. I knew he was trying to get here, but he also had to make arrangements for his cats... really Al? Cats? I also didn't want to let him know how disappointed I would be if he didn't make it. Chris told me he was working on it, and he pulled it off...again.

Chris mentioned the love back and forth with Caroline and William. They were both heavily involved with the golf outing. He talked about his loving friends who would all be in attendance. Their energy and love permeated the room. He was loved and accepted by them. And I love them for that, as does Chris. He refers to "the printer. That's me" While sitting after meditation as I write, I occasionally will hear noises emanating from the printer which is behind me. He tells me it's him. Maybe all the printers make noise when they're dormant. But it causes me to stop and listen, and I now know it's him. I had suspected it, but now I know. Chris tells me not to get caught up in worldly things and takes credit for keeping Sally and me on the same path. He makes fun of me and pushes me to finish this book. To be honest I am going full speed ahead but I have a small fear of the emptiness when this is done. But that's a worry for another day. I do feel the hugs by the way. Honest to God I do.

Chris referred to Sally and I connecting and I have to touch on that. It's very personal but I have to say that when Chris first passed, we were both devastated. Sally retreated and barely left the house for 6 months. She involved herself with thank you cards, photo's, old Instagrams and memories. I just kept pushing and would have mini breakdowns every day. It was awful. Grief is contagious and our love for our son and our loss was taking us both down. It's not that we thought about it much but we were drifting apart. But the thread that kept us together was the knowledge that the other person loved Chris so much too. Once Andrew pulled me aside and told me that Chris felt we were drifting apart and were continuing down a bad path. Andrew told me that Chris was standing next to me with his arms folded and was not pleased. He told Andrew that I needed to work on the relationship despite my grief. I needed to put in the effort… he can't do everything. It wasn't that we were doing anything conscious, but like most things at the time, it just didn't matter all that much. However, things started to shift. My love for Chris propelled me to rekindle my love for Sally. As a couple we started to come out of it a bit. And then a bit more and then even more.

I needed you to know this. I think it's part of grief. However, I think throwing in a towel prematurely is a fundamentally bad move. You can always quit…tomorrow.

Back to the outing. I was really excited about my pal Allen's reading with Andrew.

What I hoped to accomplish was that Al could connect with Debbie, maybe his mom and dad, and on the way home we would discuss the reading while I poked him occasionally for emphasis. I knew that Al was open to this world. I knew he spoke to a medium not long after Debbie's crossing. I also knew he had been on a spiritual quest since her crossing when the normal available mood altering, mind numbing substances of the day didn't deaden the pain. I knew him like I knew myself. And I knew he got it.

I picked Al up at O'Hare on Friday, Sept 8 in the morning. We drove to Milwaukee Country Club, about an hour away, while chatting it up and smoking cigars. Rather we were both chatting and I was smoking. I think his response to my offer was, "Are you crazy it's 10 o'clock in the morning." "Yeah I know," I said." Which is why we aren't going to smoke Cuban cigars yet." It made perfect sense. But I digress.

So, we arrived at Milwaukee Country Club and met up with Michael Holmberg (Uncle Mike the godfather, not uncle Mike, the breakout king who wouldn't arrive until the next day). See you're getting it, and Rick Blommer. A word about Rick. Rick runs a family chocolate business based in Chicago but does business all over the world. Every table at the annual Chris McQ outing is virtually overflowing with custom made chocolate bars and 10-pound chocolate bars are auctioned off. I have been at Penguin Players events and In Balance Ranch events where I see the evidence of Rick's good heart in the form of ten-pound chocolate bars, donated without me even knowing. When my Caroline had a recent heartbreak, she came home to 15 pounds of M&M's delivered to her apartment. He is a sweet guy and a good friend... he just looks like a jag off. (Chicago term, didn't know what it meant when I got here either).

Anyway, the four of us make up maybe the world's most enjoyable foursome, and we get together every January for a golf weekend as I've already said. I knew the fates were smiling on us as the club was serving a buffet for lunch. Nothing indicates approval from the gods like red meat and shell fish. We played our round involving lots of laughs, true fellowship, numerous cigars and I believe I won money from Allen. When he writes a book, he can tell it his way.

After showering, changing, and waiting for our dinner that never quite made it we had to hit the road. Andrew was doing me a solid by doing a reading around our schedule. So, I really wanted to be punctual. I also really wanted to play golf, relax with our pals and eat a few meals...so you get the picture. I may have tried to fit in a lot ... ya think. Also, Allen's wife Sandy, after numerous stops and delays was getting into Midway Airport (the other Chicago Airport at 10 p.m.). We decided to pick her up instead of having her rent a car, after her grueling day of travel, and Allen forgetting to take his phone off silent when she was looking to update him during the trip. Why not... we can fit that in. So, we left Milwaukee encountering rush hour around not one but two major cities. This may throw us off our heavily packed schedule. Best laid plans and all. But en-route we got a call from Andrew asking if we could push back the reading 45 minutes! "Sure buddy, we can do that. Anything for you." Was that just the way it was happening, or was there some psychic manipulation? You decide but I think Chris was moving things around to make it work. We arrived 15 minutes before the rescheduled reading and after that arrived 20 minutes before Sandy's flight landed. Too many fortunate coincidences for me to think it was random. Roll your eyes all you want, but when you buy in, you buy in. My favorite definition of coincidence is "God just showing off."

If you recall from earlier, the way Andrew works is that he requests you bring photos of the loved ones you want to contact. So, I contacted Al's sister Karen. Karen and her husband Vince were also part of my childhood. They were to Allen what my brother Jerry and sister Marcia were to me. They were role models in the truest sense. We were both blue collar kids raised by wonderful hard-working parents. But in Jerry, Marcia, Karen, and Vince we had actual role models of how to act, speak, and dress. They taught us how order off a menu and how to discreetly tip to get your way. By emulating them, we learned how to fit in a world that was unfamiliar to us. I wonder if they even knew how much we looked up to them. If not, they do now. I got to spend time with Karen and Vince at Allen's wedding the previous November and because of that I had an email to reach out to her. She sent me photos of Allen and Debbie at their wedding in 1998 that included Allen's parents…perfect.

We arrived at Andrew's with plenty of time to spare. It really is important to be able to take a few minutes to quiet your mind and try to immerse yourself in the world of spirit, prior to heading into a reading with a medium. All good, "Allen quit playing with the crystals," just kidding he was well behaved and a little nervous. I gave him the photos and I know he gave a quiet thanks to Karen. So, did I. I also know he was saying a silent prayer to Deb and his mom and dad. and so was I. I was also saying a quick prayer to Chris to come through for me, as I arranged for an hour reading, 45 minutes for Al and 15 for me and Chris. My experiences with Andrew have been so spiritually fulfilling, rewarding, and filled with validation that I hoped Al received something similar. I wanted the ride to Midway after the reading to be filled with comments like, see, yeah, right, ya know! But I've gotten ahead of myself. I presented Al with a white legal pad and a Bic Velocity pen. The type that always works for me. Andrew came out smiled warmly, looked over my shoulder and told me Chris was right behind me. He hugged me shook hands with Allen and guided him into his office.

For the next 45 minutes I hung out in Andrew's den which is more like a cosmic waiting awaiting room full of stones, books, sages etc. and chairs that are virtually impossible to get out of gracefully. Not that I do much of anything gracefully.

When Al emerged, we locked eyes. They seemed still focused on something far away and he seemed a bit shell shocked. Good I asked? "Oh my God" was his response. I smiled a little and walked into Andrew's office for my 15 minutes.

Andrew started right in after focusing on Chris over my shoulder. Andrew said that Chris is bringing up the music, songs and golf. I told Andrew about the golf outing. Andrew asked me, "Are you writing a book? Chris likes the idea and wants to be on the cover." Andrew said I had really become attuned to spirit. Andrew told me Chris was coming through so handsome. Drop dead good looking. Although his soul is aging he looks the same. He really likes the book. Andrew said he saw a billboard with words on one side and Chris' picture on the other. I said I didn't put up a billboard. "It's there, with a white background," insisted Andrew. I was getting a bit frustrated as I was sure he was on the wrong path and the clock was indeed ticking. "Concentrate. "said Andrew. "A billboard or big banner with Chris's picture, smiling on one side". Wait, you mean like a huge white banner with Chris' picture on it welcoming everyone to the outing? At this point I saw Andrew and felt Christopher roll their eyes. Yeah...really attuned.

When I rejoined Allen, he was still floating on air. We raced to the Jeep to compare readings. Both were amazing. As I've stressed, someone else' reading is very personal and his own business, but I will mention a few points to confirm the connection. Allen's wife Debbie came through and expressed her love. She also said she was very happy that Al found love again and remarried. Of course, there was a lot more that's frankly none of your business or mine. Allen's dad came through next. I knew Steve Conrad and he was a tough guy and a good man. He told Allen that he was sorry he didn't tell him he loved him growing up. He wished it were different, but that he loved him very much and is very proud of the man he grew up to be. His mom came through and expressed her love and how proud she was of him. She also told him to watch his drinking, which was something she always said to us when we were teenagers. I should have listened. :)

In the Jeep, Allen confessed that growing up, his dad rarely told him he loved him although he expressed it in other ways. Later on, well into Allen's adulthood he brought this up to his dad. Allen told me that his dad called later simply to let Al know he loved him. "No one knows about this," said my dear pal. How about that. The drive to Midway was quiet. What else was there to say?

There is something amazingly gratifying about sharing an experience like that with someone with whom you have a long history. This isn't someone from a lecture that you share a conspiratorial smile because you both get it. This is sharing a psychic experience with someone that you used to skip school with. Someone with whom you would run from the cops (one time on roller skates in Santa Monica being chased by a cop on a bicycle for skating with open containers but that's another story). Someone like you whose spiritual evolution has been propelled forward due to a devastating personal tragedy. As I write this I feel just a little smug, because both Al and I know the secret and if you've come this far in the book, hopefully you now do too. They're not gone!

So how is this possible? When we know they have crossed how can they have access us to us? But because we know that like us the ones who've crossed are energy, that may hold an answer, or more questions.

I love the book *The Secret* and it has helped pull me back from the brink of despair in various aspects of the life. The description of energy allowed me to comprehend what appeared to be incomprehensible.

The Chris McQ golf weekend went off without a hitch. All the schedules fell in place and every one (who was anyone) showed up. (just kidding). My friends shined, my kids' friends shined, and most especially, Chris' friends shined. Our family came through. After dinner I called Chris' friends to help me with a toast to my boy. It was a toast that he led his pals in often and I only learned it with his crossing over. Of course, it's an Irish toast... but aren't they all.

There are good ships and wood ships and ships that sail the sea,
but the best ships are the friendships, may they always be!"

The night ended under the stars with Frat dog playing all of Chris' favorites.

Including a soul touching rendition of *Live Like You Were Dying* and *Southern Cross.*

I cannot enough express my gratitude and love for those that helped me...helped us shoulder the burden. You know who you are. xoxox

On September 22, Chris paid a visit.

"Hi Dad, remember the beaches in Naples. You felt the angels. Well it wasn't desperation, it was real. Those were holy spots that allowed you to communicate with the other side, the other world. Just like me coming to you in Sarasota. I always wanted to be with you when I was a kid. I still do. You're not taking me away from anything. Hear that noise from the printer, that me Pop.

Remember picking me up at the airport in Buffalo. That's how it feels now. I always felt safe around you Dad. I love you Pop that's what you need to know. It's a beach Pop that's where we are connected. Barefoot on the sand. Our souls, our spirits, our beings. I miss hugging you too. When you do it I feel it crossing over to my side. The closeness, just roll with it. It's a forever thing. Don't worry so much. It's me and it's always going to be me. I'm home. Walking the grounds in Minnesota. I was so confused and tied up inside. Thanks for doing that. Thanks for the 4th of July in St. Paul. I know how much you loved me Pop...still do.

What doesn't seem real is always forever, all the time. You have that with me still. Don't let them tell you that I don't miss you on the other side. I'm very happy but I miss you! But not the pain or the sadness. I'm with you on the beach in Sarasota. You're getting older Pop. It's good. It's your path. Every day should be full, but it brings you closer to us… to me Pop.

This is a good meditation. It helps you cross across to me. Love you Pop.

Thanks for the golf outing. I was all over the place. With my friends and your friends. How it should have been. Don't think Pop, just write. Push this out to other fathers who feel empty. I do it because I love you but we need to help the broken ones Dad. Get going on it. I'm here.

Heading back…love you Dad…all the time."
Chris

This visit was truly amazing. I say that a lot but it's a perfect word for these visits.

a·maz·ing /ə'māziNG causing great surprise or wonder; astonishing.

Yeah that's the right word. I really needed to concentrate on the notes to be very clear what I transcribed. One word would change the message. And each message is so important and so precious that I can't risk being wrong. When a sentence confuses me, I usually grab a magnifying glass, (hey, I'm 61)) then say a silent prayer, sometimes not even knowing I'm praying, for clarity and wisdom. Then it comes…it really does.

Last year Andrew started to have a spirit circle the last Thursday of the month and I attended these a handful of times.

Although I did get to meet some wonderful people who are also pushing the psychic envelope, it really wasn't my cup of tea. I was really only interested in reaching Christopher. In no uncertain terms Andrew let me know that Chris was always with me at these events and that my Dad occasionally showed up with Chris. I did get something out of each reading, but I only did it to feel close to Chris. I have attended spirit circles hosted by other mediums with similar results. Lots of stuff going on here. Lots of energy. People receiving messages, people looking for validation, and some just for attention. Most of us just a little broken by a loved one's passing.

But attending groups just wasn't my thing.

During this one group though on Sept 28, 2017 I received a visit mid circle, and I began to write. (I probably missed an assignment at the reading …but that's nothing new.)

Here is what my boy said to me.

"Hi Pop, I came with you. Lots of us here tonight. I'm close. I like it better one on one but it's always me hanging with you. You crack me up because relaxing and focusing are not natural to you. Ask Andrew what I'm doing…I'm kind of laughing at you. But you know it's all good…all love. You and me Pop. You are doing a good job. You are getting it done. Keep writing, it's draining but it's worth it. When you start speaking after writing it I will always travel with you.

Clapping, smiling and hanging out with you. You know I love you Pop. It's different doing it here which means we are getting better at it. Nice going old man. New tricks…get it. Feels like twilight, bright stars and clear sky over a beach. You and me Pal. Just how I like it, remember. Just the way I liked it as a kid. You know I'd be home when you got home from work. Same thing here. Trust it Pop-Have Faith. If I can come through in Arlington Heights or

Hoffman Estates I can do it anywhere. Lighten up Andrew just busting balls a little. Andrew sees me Pop. No bullshit. Right behind you. Ask him.

Remember that night (Sarasota). I was as close as the air. You knew it. Just get used to it and accept it. I picked out the amethyst for mom. Trust me. I'm getting it done for you every day. Here and there. "

This sure doesn't need much explanation. While perusing stone and crystal jewelry in Andrews lobby I saw some beautiful bracelets for sale. Nothing caught my eye so I moved on. When I went back to it a bracelet jumped out at me. It had round black amethyst stones and I bought it for Sally. I may have paid for it but I know Chris picked it out. He was always so proud when he found just the right gift for his momma. And he did it again.

There are many types of spiritual healers. A psychic uses the five senses to connect with the deceased. A medium uses images, words and emotions. A channeler is someone who can work directly with the deceased loved one. And energy healers, they use healing that helps balance the flow of energy in your body.

One quick note about using the tools available. About a year plus in, Sally went to a psychic healer and it had an amazing effect on her spirit. A dark cloud was lifted. You could actually see it in her. For Christmas last year Sally had given me a session with the same healer on the phone scheduled the day before Chris' anniversary. Although I really anticipated something wonderful because of Sally's experience that's not what I got. I didn't like it at all, I felt uneasy, I couldn't wait to get off the phone. Not only was I uncomfortable, I was worried that this healing would break the connection with Chris and my channel writing. Of course, it didn't. The following morning on Jan 3rd Chris swung by, psychically not physically. But maybe both...

But that just goes to show you different strokes for different folks. Sally' healing was life changing and mine freaked me out. Remember what Boca said in *Mr. 3000*, "You do your thing man…just do your thing." I love that character, straight to the point, a little rough around the edges and yet somehow poignant. Reminds me of someone I know… just can't put my finger on it.

There is a really good book by my friend Jenn Weigel entitled

Psychics, Healers and Mediums. A Journalist, A Road Trip and Voices from the Other Side.

It covers the topic pretty thoroughly and clearly with a good dose of humor. My favorite kind of approach. Jen also does a great job bringing the psychic community together in the Chicago, area by bringing in mediums, channelers and healers in all different formats. She is the pied piper of the other side, and I am grateful for her friendship and guidance.

CHAPTER ELEVEN:

DUDE, WHY ARE YOU DOING THIS?

Why would you continue to put yourself in a position of reviewing a gut-wrenching loss and continued heartache? Doesn't it keep you me in the pain? That's a great question that many of you are asking. Because it does and it doesn't. The journey to finding Christopher continues on to today. It is a quandary for those who have suffer a loss of a child. Because you don't want to hurt as badly but you also don't want to break the connection. Yesterday was the first really nice day of the year. I was out with two of my best friends and we played a little golf, 40 holes to be exact. Sally went with William to a lacrosse tournament so it was just the dog and me so nothing was calling me home. After I felt pure joy and a lot of fatigue. The dog and I watched a movie and around 9pm we went to visit Chris at his grave. It was a beautiful night to sit, have a cigar and visit. On this night as there was little wind, I sent up a Chinese lantern. I began to get emotional and realized it was one part missing my son, one-part fatigue, and one-part guilt for so thoroughly enjoying the day. Even though I talked to him on the course and I knew he was around me. Not for all 40y holes…. hey, a spirit has shit to do.

The combination wore me down and I melted just a little. I was grateful that today I would be able to spend time on his book and re-engage. So yeah, going through the events of his youth and the messages of his present can be rewarding and painful at the same time. Kind of like parenting. Just kidding…exactly like parenting. And I am so grateful for the messages I've received from mediums that I will always be viewed by Chris as his father. Which is truly the greatest role I could ever ask for. And I get to keep it for eternity. See, that's the fulfilling part.

And along those lines sometimes a piece of art, or poetry, or music can perfectly describe how you feel at that moment. John O'Donohue's Benedictus on Grief is one of those pieces which is why it's included earlier.

So, I guess wrestling with "will I still be Christopher's dad on the other side" is a question that must haunt all parents who have lost kids….. But I truly know the answer now. The tears I'm shedding at this moment will be replaced with tears of joy as my Chris guides me across, and we are together again. I know that for a fact… as sure as I'm sitting here.

On September 30, 2017 Chris swung by for a brief visit.

"Hi Dad,

Remember shopping at Macy's in Tucson. I felt special and very loved. Completely focused on me. Intense love from you and mom. I know you love me & it's so very clear now. Clouded sometimes on your side but not now. It's love and it's very clear to me. I love you too. No holding back just straight back at you. Beach is how it is. All free, all energy all love. It's what works for us. Always like a Sarasota Beach at night. I miss being a kid with you. I can see it all so clearly now. Love, attention focus, and the security. I was anxious and missed some of the love. But it's not wasted. I get it all now.

Thanks for that.
Sorry you're sad pop. I'm here, hugging you, kissing you"

That really is typical of Chris' visits on this side. He would be there and we would revel in him and then he was gone, leaving us with a sort of "where'd he go feeling." Each of us who loved him still has that feeling. He talked about Tucson and shopping in Macy's. When he was graduating from In Balance we went out there and took him shopping. He was never a greedy kid wanting more of this or that. But on this day, we let him get whatever he wanted. Blazer, pants, shirts- dress and Tommy Bahama. He was just having a ball, and so were we. I can close my eyes and see that smile. He knew he was loved. Thank God he knew he was loved. The truth be told sometimes I'm just holding on (like right now). But I couldn't imagine the regret and grief I would feel if he didn't know he was so very loved.

On October 13, 2018 we went to the Wilmette Theatre to see Concetta Bertoldi. Concetta is a well-known psychic and author. It was hosted by our pal Jen Weigel and it was the exact format that we had experienced with Thomas John. Jen interviewed Concetta and she talked about her gifts and life experience using those. Then she started walking up the aisle of the theatre and engaging spirits of loved ones in the audience. She stopped at my aisle halfway up.

She said "Chris is here; who's Joe?" I told her I was. She said there was another Joe, the father and another J (Jerry) name around Chris. She also said that Joseph was part of Christopher's name.

She said Chris admired me since he was little and always wanted to be like me. Concetta said that I keep asking where are you and he keeps saying "I'm right here". I also ask why can't I see you.

Concetta said that Chris told her "I think about the things I didn't get to do. "She said he talking very fast and has a sense of humor. She said that Chris tells her I'll have a long life and he will be there to welcome you home.

She told me (us) that he died suddenly & quickly. He wants me to be happy. He said "there are girls over here too." He's not lonely or alone. He can hear what I'm saying. He's very much connected to us.

He said he can't believe how many tributes there are about him. He said his words are everywhere. He thinks it's funny that everyone "remembers all the good things but they don't remember him crashing the car."

Once again amazing... I'm not going to repeat the definition but it really is. A packed theatre full of hopeful loved ones and Chris pulls Concetta over to us. What he told her was of course spot on including my dad's name. I was so proud and so please when Concetta stated for all to hear that Chris and I had a really strong connection that couldn't be broken. When he talked of his words being everywhere I had to smile. Whenever I'm with friends or family I see wrist bands in rubber, stainless steel and silver with his words "LIFE IS HONESTLY SO BEAUTIFUL AS LONG AS YOU ALLOW IT TO BE". We wrote and perform a song with that title and it appears on a lot of screen savers. His message is everywhere, and everywhere is a better place because of it. In a short visit he confirmed through Concetta everything we've heard before. Chris made time, he came through, he warmed my heart and soul and made me smile. I would say I got what I came for...again.

CHAPTER TWELVE:

IRON JOE

This might be a good time to introduce you to the Joe who came through with Chris. He was my Dad. Chris' middle name is Joseph to honor him. Iron Joe (his nickname on the railroad) was, in my opinion, one of the finest men to walk the earth. He was flawed as are we all, but he was full of love, at least and maybe only for his family. My Dad started working after his father died when he was still in grammar school, and he soon became the bread winner for the family. He drove a horse drawn wagon making deliveries in Buffalo for Lang's Bakery. Later, he ended up on the railroad and had a second job filling vending machines. My dad was a union man through and through and that meant something then. I even remember Dad keeping a lead pipe in his car in case there were union troubles. See what I mean - Iron Joe.

But like most Irish fathers, my Dad was sentimental and emotional when it came to his kids. Sundays was a mandatory meal at the McQuillen home. Even after the older kids were married they would show up on Sunday with their own brood for dinner, touch football and a family game of cards or charades. On special occasions and holidays, my Dad would give a toast after grace (which he himself didn't say). I think he was mad at God but the reason was none of our business. I guess God mended fences with the Old Man as I know they are together now.

The toast was always the same - "To my family" - a toast he barely completed as Iron Joe would choke up as he tried to say those words. I have often felt that my belief in God came easier to me because I had such a loving father. I knew that my Dad wanted the best for me and would move heaven and earth to keep me safe and make me happy. I could tell so many stories about my Dad. He would sit down to dinner and survey the table, laying eyes on a pal who came to dinner or in Allen Conrad's case, stayed the summer. "Hey you," asked my dad, "are you one of mine?" "No sir, said my pal would respond, "I'm Allen." "Well that's good, now get your elbows off the table"." He had the ability to bark at you while simultaneously making you feel loved. It was his love language. My friends loved my Dad.

The story of the blended family was handed down to me by my older siblings and my parents, though I didn't really know about it until my mom filled me in when I was in sixth grade. In December of 1956, my Uncle Gene (who was my dad's younger brother) and Aunt Doll (who was my mom's younger sister) were involved in a horrible car accident that took my Aunt's life and left their five children motherless and petty banged up. The story goes that the five kids were taken in by various aunts and uncles. One by one the kids began showing up and staying at our house. And that was that. The family of five just became a family of ten. Uncle Gene had been drinking on that fateful evening and that was the cause of the crash. He was allowed to stay with us as long as he abstained from alcohol. But he didn't stay sober long. What happened next soon became folklore and I didn't know until a few years ago if it was legend or fact. But my sister Marcia said she was present and it happened. The story goes Gene came home drunk and my Dad (our Dad now) greeted him at the top of the stairs with a shot gun and announced he was going, one way or another. That was Iron Joe. He was now father to all the kids and Mom was mother to everyone and we were brothers and sisters, and that was that. There was no formal adoption or state assistance. We took care of our own. The only two who didn't know about the accident when it happened was my sister Debbie and me. I wasn't yet born and Debbie was a baby. My parents finally broke down and told Debbie on the eve of her high school graduation from Mount Mercy Academy. But that was Iron Joe. He worked, coached baseball, tipped a few longnecks (maybe more than a few) and loved his family. That's why I'm not surprised that my Dad is looking after Chris and showing up in the background just to let me know he's around.

One quick story about my Dad after he crossed. I was in the midst of managing a struggling business and running myself ragged with stress and worry. One night while saying a prayer I asked my Dad how he kept it together raising ten kids. I went to sleep and the next morning as I was leaning over the wash basin in the master bathroom, I saw something shiny. There on the counter next to the basin was an UTU (United Transportation Union) lapel pin in cellophane. I called out and asked Sally if she placed it there or knew where it came from. She had no idea. But I did... I got the message. "I love you, I'm here, and be a man." I had left the railroad in 1980, a good 20 years before and probably lived in a dozen places in several states. But there it sat on my bathroom sink in Winnetka, Illinois. Thanks Dad. By the way... I still have that pin. This event happened just as I wrote it, just like that.

I have always given Dad all the credit for uniting the family but none of this could have been done without my mom. She gave up any semblance of a normal life to raise ten kids. Lunches, laundry, grocery shopping and loving. Bandaging, hugging and sometimes harboring us from inquiring police or hostile neighbors. That was Rita, that was my mom. My mom adored me and I have often felt her around the nursery when each of my three took their turn in the outrageously overpriced Bellini crib. I love you, mom...thanks.

Ten days later on October 24, 2017 Chris woke me up for a visit.

"Where ya been, Pop? I've been waiting for you. Getting old Pop. How's my book? Put time aside. Time to dig in. Lots of graduations and moving on both sides. My life on your side would have changed, dramatically different. Happy here. Safe, no stress, no fear, no anxiety. Just good, warm and loved. You guys did a good job. Please believe that. Believe it. Take a breath. Somethings shifting for you and it's good. You're starting to accept the path. How it is. Lots to learn. I did it all at once. I'm walking you through it ahead of time. You'll be prepared. I was surprised but not shocked. A good surprise like Christmas. I didn't really think too much ahead of time. It's like waking up and saying 'oh man, I get it.' Get the book going. Ask ahead of time and I'll be around to help. It will help people and that's a big part of what we do. How you get here. Loans don't matter, deals don't matter. What you did matters. Loving me the way you did matters. Pure love. I came through to Concetta for you. She took her time getting to you but damn if I wasn't steering her to you. You knew it. You expected it. I wouldn't let you down Pop. Good crystal in your hand pop. It's an energy magnet. Always hold it when we visit. The dog sees me. She thinks it's normal. She's right here, Pop.

I like the research. We'll pull this off. So humble-stay humble. It matters. We're all pulling for you here, but you only call on me so they stay back. You'll visit on the journey but for now it's just you and me Pop. 'Just the way I like it.' I know it's not your favorite analogy but the journey is like a canoe ride sliding through the water gently and gracefully. Smooth ride…that's what over here is. Smooth, warm and safe. I really love it. I miss you though, they are wrong about that. We can love the now and appreciate it. But still miss the ones we love so much. I missed you in Tucson and DeKalb and I miss you here. I look back and see how strong your love was and is Pop. Thanks for that. I love you too. Think about when I was a kid and we would be laying on your bed watching TV. That kind of connection, and pure love. That's here. That's why

I'm waiting for you. We can share this which is fucking awesome.
I don't swear as much as before but....

    Good session Pop, good visit. I am always with you. Catch me
in the corner of your eye. It's me, Pop and I love you. "

Pulling Back
Love Chris

Well, he did it again. He really is amazing. He busts my stones
and pushes me to finish this book. He also lovingly lets me know
that he is waiting on the other side for me and that he isn't going
anywhere. Originally, I feared that we would cross paths between
worlds. I was afraid that I would cross over while he was on his
way back to this side. I know it sounds a bit silly but it was a fear.
It isn't now. I know for a fact that he is letting me know that he
is waiting for me and will walk me across. He also lets me know
that his presence will make my transition smoother than his and
I ought to be grateful. I am. I have been told that the shortest
span of time on the other side (our time as theirs is based on
space time continuum) which I will get to, is eighty years. This
fact was very reassuring to me and quelled my fears of crossing
paths with Chris. I have been told by a number of mediums
that Chris was an old soul and he may not be coming back.
Once again, pretty reassuring stuff. Maybe the song by Chris'
pals the DuPont Brothers wrote about him entitled *Stay Put* was
about this very thing. I was also told by Nancine long ago that
my Dad had a tough life on this side and was also done. Once
again, good news for me.

One more fast-forward. I am in Naples Fla., visiting my sister and Chris' godmother Marcia. She has been diagnosed with cancer and in the midst of making some decisions on her future. She is constantly surrounded by her two adoring adult kids and her grandchildren. She spends most of her time with either her son Norman in Houston where she receives cancer treatment, or with her daughter Colleen in northern VA. Colleen and her husband Dave bought a house big enough to accommodate Marcia and their three kids. Both Chris and I adore Marcia and have always felt her as a pure source of love and acceptance in our lives. It was so nice to have her to ourselves for a few days. We sit and talk, then eat (me, not her) then talk some more. Our conversations are deep; we talk of life and beyond. We talk of family, this book and our adored Christopher. She would need to rest between visits and I would do some editing. This is the only place outside of my office where I have worked on my book.

I won't let the notes of his visits out of my office, for fear they would somehow get lost or destroyed. Because of her love for both of us I find myself letting go and weeping often with her. On the second day of my three-day visit, after a take-out dinner and a movie, Marcia went to bed. I drove down toward the Naples Pier to walk out on the beach and try to connect with Chris. I sat on the sand and tried to meditate but I couldn't connect or so I thought. I didn't really feel I made contact. However, I did see a yellow flash of light out of the left side of my eye. And then it happened again. I really didn't think much of it and felt disappointed that I didn't feel Chris in that familiar setting. That is until I was editing the previous visit from Chris that ended with "catch me in the corner of your eye. It's me Pop and I love you." Oh, ye of little faith.

Chris talks about graduation on both sides. I am convinced there are many levels on the other side, and I have been told that, for lack of a better term, Chris is a great student and has moved up quickly since crossing over. He acknowledged that his life on this side was about to get bumpy and he seems happy to have sat out that ride. As for Concetta, he is letting me know that he herded her over my way. That's my boy.

He talks about a canoe as an analogy of life on the other side. This is further evidence that the words are not mine. Trust me, I would never use a canoe analogy, never. He's gentle and sweet and funny…he's still my Christopher.

On November 4, 2017 at 3:17a.m. Chris connected with me.

"Hi Dad, (you're) going in the right direction. It's all new to you but I'm proud of you. You're open and getting it. Lots to do, lots to figure out. Whole new world… brand new.

Feel the energy that's the whole deal. Energy-that's a sign that's it's on. When you finally figure out that it's just a short run, you start to figure out that it's not that important. Except the love and the kindness. That's what matters. That moves the whole world. You may not know it but you are doing just fine. Gives you a purpose right. You and me. I am waiting here. Time doesn't matter. Blink of an eye. That's what you say, Pop. Don't blink.

Get Will (William) in the space. Maybe Thomas John for both of them. Work today. Both need to know I'm not gone. I'm waiting. I did love them both. My selfishness was insecurity. You know how sensitive I was, more than you know. Alcohol put it on the shelf.

Caroline is so deep that her pain is just below the surface. Not just because I'm gone but she didn't know why I didn't show her love on your side. I didn't know how. I couldn't validate her world or I was a failure. I'm so sorry, selfish and so sorry. I'll make it up to you from here and guide and protect her. To be in her world. I'm all around her but she doesn't feel me. She needs to let go like falling off a cliff.

Lots of good stuff today. (But) I'm still getting all the attention. Turn it on them both.

Keep focused on the book. Too cold to golf, so dive in. I'll help. Plus, I'm around you when you write so it's good for our connection. I love being with you Pop. Always did, always will. Even when you cross over you're my Dad. I love you and that doesn't change in another dimension. Deeper Dad; Don't be afraid to go deeper. Get back to that beach Dad. You know the one —crystal isn't it? Now focus on the work we have to get done.

Thanks Dad, I like it when you kiss my picture. I feel it across the field. I get it. It's not one way.

Jerry is here. Tell Karen, Mike and Kathy. Maureen already knows and that they will be together. Good strong love there. I love you Pop, the rest is all bullshit. One journey.

It's heaven, it's my reality. All the time. All one. Like a perfect vacation. Perfect, like the first day at Vanderbilt Beach, first day on the cruise, first day on Captiva. But that's every day Pop. Friggin' amazing. Keep working on this. I'm proud of you.

Caroline is sleep walking a little. The more she feels me, the less she will hurt.

I'll help. That's the message from Thomas. He's like a cosmic amazon prime. … That's funny."

Love you Pop…going back
Chris, I love you
Found the glasses right. ☺

Jesus, Mary, Joseph, Patrick and all the Saints (no blasphemy intended), did that visit cover a lot. He prompts me to finish this book and lets me know I'm getting open. He also talks about his relationship with his sister. As I've already said, he was not a good big brother. He was getting better and rallied a few times but on the whole his actions on this side left both kids wondering why their big brother didn't approve of them. He let me know (and now you) that the reason he couldn't be a good big brother was due to his insecurity and desire to protect himself. Both kids were able to function in the main stream world but Chris struggled there. To validate their success and even existence was to admit his failures. This is a huge revelation from the other side. This is also tough to write about and think about as to reflect on his pain here is troubling.

I love how he talked about heaven and that his reality being like a perfect vacation. To be accurate, he said it was like the first day of a perfect vacation. Perfect! Spring break with my kids was my favorite week of the year. We usually went somewhere tropical, often including a visit to Aunt Marcia's in Naples, and then on to a beach hotel or resort. With three kids, Florida is about as tropical as you get. I loved every minute (except trying to get the fudgesicle stains out of Marcia's white couch, or carpet, or trips to urgent care for ear infections, etc). Actually, I even loved those moments. I remember taking Caroline out in the stroller around 2 a.m. on Captiva Island when she was about three-years-old and had a bronchial infection. The warm, heavy air did her good and I loved the one-on-one time. I loved spring break because it was the one week I would wake up with my kids and put them to bed. We found a place north of Naples called the Vanderbilt Beach Inn. It was a resort built in a horseshoe design with hotels rooms around the palm tree lined pool and Gulf efficiencies right on the beach, and a Tiki Shack for food and music. For maybe five years in a row, we would stay there in an efficiency. Five of us in one sort of big room. We stopped going only when the building was torn down and replaced with multi-million dollars high rise condos. But we made the most of it and our time there. After landing in Ft. Myers, we would pull our rental van into the Walgreen's parking lot and load up on beach toys, sun screen, cereal, and flashlights (for flashlight tag on the beach at night). We would drive a couple of miles to Vanderbilt beach and check in. We would then throw our stuff in the room, jump on the beds (mandatory), put on swimsuits and hit the beach, then pool, then beach, then Tiki Shack and then... well you get it. My God I loved those days. If Chris is right and heaven is like the first day of spring break then sign me up. Maybe this book will help me get in.

Chris talked about Caroline, not allowing herself to let him in. One day I was sitting in a coffee shop with Jen Weigel discussing my book. Thomas John called her about some scheduling issue and she mentioned she was with me. He said to say hi and when I was heading for my jeep, I got a text message that she was relaying to Caroline, from Chris through Thomas (just read again and it will make sense.) It's her message but it was spot on. Which is why Chris referred to Thomas as a cosmic Amazon prime. Jeez, he's still a really funny kid.

Well, I guess we are rounding third. Which is what I say about where I am in life. In the book we've (Chris and I) have made the turn and halfway home. I am now at my last medium reading of 2017. I have six more visits from Chris involving the channel writing. You see this is about my two-year journey since Chris crossed over and it will end on the second anniversary of that crossing on January 3, 2018.

I've continued on after of course but midway through the book I was told this is where it would end. And I've learned to follow direction. I believe my search will continue until Chris walks me across, but until then the visits are just part of my life. And for that I am humble and grateful. As recently as 3 a.m. this morning he came and I wrote. I also stumbled on an amazing guided meditation. Chris and I also agreed to meet at his grave this morning. I need you, and I mean I need you to understand something about these visits at the grave. They aren't sad, or poignant, or profound. It's simply a chance to sit with my son and chat where the energy is conducive to communication from the other side

On Saturday November 25, Jen was sponsoring a reading session with Sheri Jewel, the medium we had met last June. I didn't think I could make it to the session as I had been bird hunting with my brother- in-laws out in a far western suburb. But with my dog in the back, Buffett on the stereo and a cigar in my mouth I raced to the reading. Oh yeah, I forgot to mention that I didn't rsvp or make a reservation, but something in my head said go. So, I did. When I walked in the Winnetka Bottle Shop, reeking of Romeo & Julieta cigar smoke and sporting a camo hat, I was warmly welcomed. Despite being all female, with nary a bird hunting cigar smoker among them, they greeted me warmly. I was however told by my pal Jen that Sheri was booked full and they were very close to wrapping it up. But my instinct told me to hang in there. I had nothing to lose. So, I hung in.

I have always been a big fan of hanging in there and seeing what happens. Things usually work out if you just hang in there. Let me give you an example. In December of 2009 my old pal Rich and I decided to take our boys on a hockey road trip. Rich and I played hockey together and have been friends since the mid -1980s when two roommates dumped us. We had both moved to the north shore and raised our kids there. Our youngest boys, then nine-years-old, played hockey together. We decided to surprise them with a trip to Buffalo and Toronto as their Christmas present. Rich and Jeremy picked up William and I and we headed for the airport. They had no idea what to expect. We landed in Buffalo and headed for Niagara Falls (the Canadian side, always the Canadian side). We stood there watching the falls. After a meal at Hoaks restaurant on the lake we headed to HSBC Arena to watch the Sabres play The Blackhawks. The McQ's in their Sabre jerseys (called sweaters if you are Canadian) and the Kaspers in their Hawks gear.

It was a great game and the Sabres actually won, honest... look it up. We crashed at my brother's house and in the morning drove the hour and a half to Toronto. We checked into a hotel right near the Leaf Center and we were planning to take in the Hockey Hall of Fame. When checking in we were chatting about how smoothly everything was going up to this point when the very sweet hotel clerk told us that we could check in early, leave late tomorrow and did we want four complimentary tickets to the Hall of Fame? Thanks-thanks and yes, we replied.

We took in the hall and watched the Maple Leafs play the Capitals that night. When the game was over we were hanging around the rink as rink rats do and as we started to head back to the hotel I noticed a number of people assembling all wearing lanyards… a sure sign something was up.

I asked an usher and he said that it was a special holiday meet and greet for VIP's with the Maple Leaf players. "Dude, "I said to Rich, "we need to get in. "I asked the usher how do we make this work? "Aw, man … no way," he replied. I then asked who was in charge of the event. He pointed to a woman a blazer who was just bit older than us. The usher was grateful to pass me off to his supervisor. I approached Marie and asked her if we could participate. And of course, she said no. I then explained that we traveled far from the great city around Lake Michigan with our boys who were die-hard Maple Leaf fans to see their heroes in person as a Christmas gift. I gave the boys the nod and they began to absolutely beam, decked out in their brand-new Maple Leaf Jerseys. "After all, Marie… it is Christmas." "Okay," she said. "

Just go stand over there and I'll get you in "I began to gather my troops and Rich was missing. "Where is your Goddam father?" I growled to Jeremy. When you are sneaking in, jumping fences and crashing a party, timing is everything. You don't want to anger the crashing gods or make Marie look for you. Jeremy found his dad and balance was restored.

Marie waved us in and we were in a small room adjacent to the dressing room. The players and coaches began to come out and mingle with the VIP's and the small band of American frauds. This is where the wheels began to wobble and Marie began to catch on. As suited strapping young man would come into the room we would look to Marie to let us know if he was a player. She would nod her head if it was a player and the boys would politely approach the player for an autograph on their Leaf's jersey. The jig was up but Marie good- naturedly continued to point out players and coaches and the boys set upon them like

hyenas to get their autographs and photos. William's Leaf Jersey
about half the size of his current jersey hangs in the closet behind
my desk to this day, full of Leaf's autographs. We flew home
to Chicago the next day in time to watch the Blackhawks beat
the Lightning at the United Center. What a whirlwind, what a
weekend. A Little while later Rich asked me, "Hey back there
in Toronto, you seemed to sense we would get in, how did you
know?" I said "It's a gift really. When Marie told us to beat it,
even when she said it a couple of times, her heart really wasn't
in it. "Thanks Marie, you made two young faux Maple Leaf fans
and their dad's pretty happy that night.

Now back to the event at Wilmette Bottle Shop with Sheri Jewel. I was sitting on a couch with all women, with either psychic gifts themselves or somehow connected to the psychic world. Not only was I the only male, I was dressed like one of the inbred stars of Duck Dynasty and smelled of gunpowder and cigar smoke. I tried to blend in which didn't work so I closed my eyes and tried to make myself small. That didn't work either so I just hung in there.

Jen came over and apologized for not being able to fit me in. It was the end of the session; the shop was closing and the medium was tired. Oh yeah, they had reservations at the Italian restaurant down the street pretty soon and as it was Saturday night so they had to be on time. With the odds stacked completely against me, I knew just what to do, hang in.

You need to understand that the odds have always been against me. At only 160 pounds, I was a starting lineman on the high school football team. I am not all that good looking and I married the prettiest girl I knew and we have been married over a quarter of a century. I was the last guy you ever would bet on to get sober, and I've been sober for 32 years now. We have a saying in AA: don't give up five minutes before the miracle. You know what that means to me, don't you? Hang in there!

So that's exactly what I did. I hung in there.

Sheri walked back into the middle of the shop from the front alcove where she was reading spirits. "Well," she said, "You're here, and Chris is here and I'm here so let's go talk to him."

See you gotta hang in there....

"He said Happy Holiday. "I heard cross; do you have a cross? "I was wearing my Celtic Cross which was quite similar to the one Chris wore. Sheri said that Chris is really good at talking.

She tells me that Chris is saying that I'm starting to make more sense out of a project. (this one)

It's going to become clearer. His picture will be on the cover. He's saying that you were his best friend. Obviously, he loves you. Sheri touched her temple and said, "aneurysm.... who is that?"

It was my niece Kerry. "She's here too. They are together on the other side. He's an old soul"

Sheri said Chris needs me to know and I know you know said Sheri that he's okay. But you need to believe it more. He watches over you. He's never going away. Sheri said that Chris does have work to do. He's working with children on the other side. Has anyone ever told you that? Helping kids…He's like a guide to them.

He says he misses you terribly still. But you need to know that you are going to be ok. He said "His mom is doing better than you." "Do you know someone who had a heart attack?" asked Sheri. I answered my Dad did. Your Dad is here too, here to support. Coming together for holidays. Focus on good memories. You're adjusting better than you used to do, said Chris.

She said Chris was bringing up pinewood derby. He's bringing up jumping into pools on vacation. Sheri said that's she's not saying Chris was a bad boy but that he liked to live on the edge. He said to say he's sorry but he couldn't do it any other way. There are lessons to learn from it. She told me Chris had a really good heart.

Sheri said he was showing her difficulty in swallowing because he drowned. She said he told her he had a quick death and he didn't suffer. Water was cold and he was drunk. Boom, out go the lights. He didn't suffer. It's really important to him that you know that.

He said, "Blink of an eye…. then gone." He said he hoped knowing that took some of the pain away. Tell mom that too. None of the kids suffered. "Boom & over." There were other drugs involved. Sheri said, "I see a Mad Hatter which means all

206

MY SEARCH FOR CHRISTOPHER ON THE OTHER SIDEMY SEARCH FOR CHRISTOPHER ON THE OTHER SIDE

kinds of drugs." He told her he's in a better place & loves what
he's doing now. Sheri confided that he later may have committed
suicide if this didn't happen. Not would have for sure though.
Too much up and down and a really hard life for him. She said
Chris wouldn't take back anything he did, but he's so glad it's
over. He was tormented and very sensitive.

She asked about burying him. He said it wouldn't have mattered to him but it makes me feel better. Sheri said Chris told
her I have a bracelet from him (Goofy Bracelet).

Chris told her that I was the best dad he could ever have.
Forgive yourself…it doesn't matter.

Sheri said I now have a better understanding and am more
compassionate.

"When you are stargazing," she said. "He's with you." He's
mentioning an uncle (probably Jerry). Sheri said Chris liked to
party the way I used to party. But he was frustrated and had
some anger. Chris said, "I was a mixed-up kid." Sheri told me
he's really good looking and a much wiser soul. She looked at me
and asked, "Are you counting the days until you see him?" Chris
told her, "No dad, you have a lot of life to live. You won't suffer."

Sheri told me that I am between two worlds and I have to
keep the balance. "Remember you have a family here." Your
story will be told, she said. Christopher's story.

Sheri asked me what's with the stairs and I explain I kiss
his picture on the way down. He knows that she said. She told
me to work with my third eye. She told me he's acknowledging
my ears and prayers. He's telling you, "It's okay, Dad," but you
don't hear him. He's telling her necklace but she's not sure why.

She said Chris is showing her a plate of food. "Did you
make him a plate of food?" I had to smile thinking of the plate
I prepared of roast beef and corn for the frat brothers stranded
in DeKalb.

Chris told Sheri that he will be there for Christmas. She said my Dad has his arm around Christopher. "I got the kid," said Iron Joe. Sheri told me that my dad keeps him in line.

She asked if my Dad smoked cigarettes and drank beer. Did he ever, like half a case of beer at a sitting and two packs a day. "Was your Dad a baseball fan?" Yeah, he was.

Sheri said Chris had a beautiful smile and was an all-American boy.

Sheri ended with, "You have more surprises coming. A Journey, seeing things and hearing things. You need to *F@#%ing Practice*".

Well, Sheri don't play. And she didn't hold back. If you take away only two thoughts from this book:

They are not gone

Sometimes you just have to hang in there

If I didn't hang in then I wouldn't have gotten this amazing visit from Chris through Sheri Jewel.

Oh my God, he got right down to it. From depression, to the actual drowning incident to being with his cousin Kerry and my Dad. Sheri asked if I made him a plate of food. Really, only Chris and I knew what a significant gesture that was. It was without a doubt a gesture I made out of love for him.

Chris talks about the book; he talks about our bond and he reprimands me to stay in the now. Tomorrow will take care of itself. But he knows how much I miss him and he knows how much I loved and still love him. I am touched to know that he *"misses me terribly."* And for all that I am terribly grateful to Chris and to Sheri. As the last medium session of 2017 and the last one for this book, it sure was a powerful one.

I ask each medium who connects with Chris. Can you see him, what does he look like and can you hear him? Does he send signs?

CHAPTER THIRTEEN:

THERE ARE MORE
THINGS IN HEAVEN AND EARTH

"There are more things in heaven and earth,
Horatio, Than are dreamt of in your philosophy."
–Hamlet (1.5.167-8), Hamlet to Horatio

You've just read the last medium reading and I have seven more visits from Chris up to and including Jan 3, 2018. I must admit that I'm a little scared. I've been writing this book for more than a year and accumulating data for nearly two and a half years. That will continue, as will my research, search and most importantly, his visits. I have just scratched the surface and I need to continue this big leap of love and of faith. I have to keep looking because I'm not sure I can exist in a world devoid of Christopher. This book has been an anchor for me as is the golf outing. It is a significant project. I will finish this soliloquy of mine at the end of this book. But know I will miss talking to you.

On November 26, 2017, just a few hours after sitting with Sheri, Chris came through.

"The light (moonlight) coming in the window reminds me of Florida, a year ago. Sarasota is sacred. Find more sacred places. Research and find them. I'm around you, Pop. I came through with Sheri last night. Lots of family for the holidays. Good job writing the book. I'm moving your hand here and helping you write the book. It's sad on our side here when the kids can't connect with their parents. They don't know the door is open to them. They think they are just gone. Spread the word in your way, pop. Good job. We are picking up momentum. We are closer because of it. I know that's the motive. It raises consciousness when you can wake parents up. You can navigate both worlds and because of who you are people will listen.

I'm not going anywhere. Be aware of me around you. Lights flashing like lightning in the distance. Come by the grave today and take a load off, Pop. I will be there for you. Go Bills! It still matters but only because it matters to you. Smell the sage; it reminds you of me, you know, like my bedroom.

I love you too, Pop, but you have work to do. It will bring you closer to me and raise up the consciousness. All good Dad.

It's like when I would come home from Tucson. I knew you would be there so know I will be here when you cross. I told you. I may even be done coming back, at least for now. Not sure. But going nowhere until we are together. When you came to Arizona was I there. Same thing, Pop.

Working on a lot of things like school, but it's all really clear and uplifting. Different levels. You'll see.

I was at the Ranch with you. But don't get hung up on places. I'm wherever you go.

Good music. To me it's vibrations and I really like it. That rainbow was for you. You're not making this up. Don't doubt.

When you tell people about this, about us, you can look in their eyes and see if they get it. If they can't, don't waste your time. You'll see a spark -that's the one. They need the message.

I miss golfing with you. It's not cold here, never cold here. Think of mid 70's with a warm breeze. Now think of that forever. No rain-no cold. Good deal all around.

You're pretty aware Pop, pretty open. I know you're worried about running out of things to say but we never did and we never will. It's just us talking. I love you so. Real clear now, like I can see love. Like a colored wave or a blue breeze. See there are some things they don't know. Let 'em scratch their heads."

Love you Pop
Chris

Where do I start with this visit? He not only encourages me in a new direction but tells me why. It's the parents of the kids who don't know what we know. Although we can't see them (at least most of us can't) they are not gone. It was so like Chris to break things down to the simplest format or explanation. "Was I here when you came to visit in Tucson? And then he tells me he'll be right there when I cross. But he also wants me to be present on this side. To stay in the NOW. The hereafter will take care of itself. The rest of the visit is self-explanatory. He makes it clear.

On either side of the veil though, Chris seems to expect me to be able to "get it done." No matter what it is. He may be giving me too much credit as usual but I will do my best for you Chris. Anything for you.

Several terms have been used recently that I think are worth defining. I keep hearing and writing about consciousness. it is an important concept so here's my definition:

Consciousness - *the state of being awake and aware of one's surroundings*

Higher consciousness… *is the consciousness of a higher Self, transcendental reality, or God.*

We have been told by virtually every medium that we utilized that Chris was an old soul. We somehow intuitively knew what that meant. Here is what I mean by old soul. Old souls are said to be souls that have experienced reincarnation many times and retain a wisdom gained from those past lives.

Chris came through for a short visit on December 2, 2017 at 4:30 a.m.

"You need to stay closer, Pop. Almost two years but that's your time. I know you miss me and I miss you too, but I'm really good. This won't end on the anniversary Dad; don't worry about it. We're stuck with each other. Just you and me, remember. I'm never alone, never lonely. I'm always around you all the time. All the way till you're back home. I'm writing the book with you. I'm going to be at the grave today when my friends come. Strong bond there. Lots of love.

It was me with Sheri Jewel last week; I was remembering fishing in Florida. That really made me happy. I love you, Pop. You did a good job…lighten the f@#$ up. I'm great. I'm glad to help you with the deal. I do what I can. I told you not to worry about it. It worked out, right? Have faith in me, Pop."

My goodness, he mentions Florida and fishing and I'm back on that skiff with my two boys' backwater-fishing. I grew up across the street from Lake Erie so I did some fishing growing up but the sport never grabbed me. But my boys, especially my oldest, loved it and if we were anywhere near water, like on our Florida trips, it was top of the list of things to do. Chris came by his A.D.D. through his Dad, so I got him. When he was little, Sally and I attended a lecture on A.D.D. which was a new subject that was just starting to be addressed. The speaker made a big impression on me when he said, "To understand a kid with A.D.D. you had to grasp that there were two kinds of time.... now & not now. "The light bulb went off for me. We were in Ft. Lauderdale waiting to board a Royal Caribbean Cruise Ship the next day. As with most vacations I let each kid pick one major activity. On the way back to the hotel after dinner, maybe three hours after landing in Ft Lauderdale, Chris played his chit. We were passing a marina with charter boats just getting in or preparing for the morning's charter. Tomorrow wouldn't do as we had to board the cruise ship mid-morning. I was now negotiating with a skipper for an evening charter. Several hundred bucks later we were heading out to open waters. Of course, we had a ball, and if I recall, caught nothing. But my Chris was happy. And that was enough for me. We docked smelling of fuel and bait and headed for the hotel.

We had another fishing adventure during spring break of 2009. Caroline's school break came later so only the boys and I were down there. We chartered a boat and fished the backwaters of the island and my boys were in heaven. Casting out and pulling in fish, while their old man sat in a swivel chair smoking a cigar hoping I didn't get a strike. We fished for hours and as I write this I'm back on that little skiff with my 9 year old and my 14 year old. When it was time to return to the marina, the captain told us about a joint on the water that would cook our catch. We convinced him to join us and we grabbed a table. My Chris was so proud when he went to the kitchen with his Amber Jack catch to tell the cook how he wanted it prepared. We sat under the thatched roof and watched the sun come down and the water roll by. There was a singer hitting the stage with his guitar and guess what, he played a medley of Jimmy Buffett songs. It could not have been better. We ate Chris' catch, hummed and sang along and I took it all in. Even then I knew that this moment was special and would mean something later on.

CHAPTER FOURTEEN:

God Called Him Home Early

I think it's time to write about a subject I don't want to write about. And I probably wouldn't write about it other than it coming up in the last medium session.

Which means it came from Christopher. And it was part of our reality. Even in my first visit with Andrew, he told me that despite his party boy demeanor that there were times Chris didn't want to be here.

The thought of this scared his mother and me, and probably scared Chris. When he went back to drinking and the darkness would creep in, I was scared to death that I would get a call. You see we are Irish, and unless you are Irish, it's hard to know what that entails. As the late Daniel Patrick Moynihan said, "To be Irish is to know that in the end the world will break your heart."

That's what it means. Mix alcohol with a dark poet's soul and you get a Eugene O'Neil play. A fucking heart-breaking tragedy.

It's genetic and it runs like a thread though some families, like ours. We were full of laughter, warmth and love but there was the thread. Patrick, my dad's father, started the tradition. He hung himself when my dad was a boy. I guess he drank too much and family legend has it that his wife liked the nightlife and all that goes with it. We never talked about it, and certainly never asked Dad about it. The story was just passed on. When my brother Bobby returned from Atlanta in the middle of the night, and then just stayed, we never talked about it much. Before that, when he showed up, having left his seminary studies, we didn't talk about it at all. We were good at keeping secrets and letting each other keep theirs. We never really talked much about the accident in 1956 either come to think of it. We banded together and we moved on.

In the spring of 1977 as a sophomore in college I was in Ft. Lauderdale for spring break. I took a train down as flying was out of the question, and as a railroad kid, my travel by train was free. My buddy Bobby Marx (whose dad was a judge from Rochester) could have flown down with our other pals but he chose to take the train with me. We had planned on a week of complete debauchery. It was a good plan. We found our pals; the hotel room that they had was full so the first night we slept in the laundry room, but we couldn't have cared less. It was beaches, beer, tanning oil and palm trees. It was heaven. A few days into the trip someone found my friend Bobby who then found me to say there was a family tragedy and I had to call home. My 29-year-old brother Bobby had hung himself. My brother Paul found him, and of course we never talked about it. Bobby's note mentioned being gay, which I never knew. But the reality was that it was the alcohol. That monster had taken him. He had mentioned someone he loved, and my conservative blue-collar family rose to the occasion and embraced his partner like a lost member of the family. The Catholic Church was pretty strict back then and people who committed suicide were not supposed to be entitled to a mass or a burial in hallowed ground. But the young priest from St. Joe's, our childhood parish, paid no heed. To this day I am grateful to that representative of Christ. He handled Bobby's premature death by saying that, "God called him home early." Forty plus years later I can recall those words and am grateful to that priest.

A few years before, after a drunken brawl with his dad, my Uncle Bill, out of guilt and fueled by alcohol, tried to hang himself with the dog's leash. Thank god, the leash broke and Uncle Bill, ashamed and a little worse for wear, got on with his life. This guy was a giant. A man among men. He looked like Dean Martin, was a war hero in the Pacific and a semi pro football star, and of course a railroader. How could things be so bleak that a dog's leash seemed like an answer? That's the thread.

In 1993, my brother Billy's life ended at 49 in a car crash. Billy had been drinking when his sports car crashed into a wall. Billy had been a Marine Corps Lieutenant who served in Vietnam, a presidential appointee at 33 and later a trial attorney in Texas. But despite his early successes alcohol had always played a role in his story. His crash was ruled as an accident and we never talked about it but there is the thread.

At the end of my drinking while circling the drain I myself left a poetic suicide note after taking a bunch of pills and washing them down with a Budweiser. I lay down on the weight bench in my living room after doing a few reps. I awoke the next morning to someone pounding on my door to remind me of the lunch date we had with a couple of gals at Murphy's Irish Pub in Old Town. Oh well, I guess the show must go on. However, I did get sober not long after that and I began to try to break the thread.

Now you understand that our concerns about Chris and the pain of depression, treated by alcohol, was rooted deeply in my family. That is why in almost every reading with a medium, Chris makes it very clear that what happened was a dumb, tragic accident. It was absolutely not a continuation of the tragic family tradition.

I didn't want to write this chapter. There is a feeling of disloyalty when opening up these doors and letting you look in. But as I was driving to work yesterday I had this urge to turn around and write this while the feeling was fresh. But I couldn't write at home where our floors were being done. I also didn't want to write this section sitting in my office in the city. Every word, every key stroke of this book was written at my desk, in my office at home, that was Christopher's bedroom. I know his spirit moves in and around easily in this space. I feel his spirit and his inspiration. I know I will finish this book where I started it, at my desk in Chris' room, with his spirit traveling back and forth across the divide.

(Note: I finished this book where I started it in my office that was Chris' bedroom. But I felt Chris around me in Florida at Marcia's home and by the pool Chris so loved that I felt compelled to do some editing and small additions on my most recent visit. If just felt right.)

Just so you know. This chapter nearly overwhelmed me with grief, powerlessness, fear and loneliness. I miss my dysfunctional but loving childhood. I miss my parents and my siblings who have crossed. I miss my sweet charming loving Uncle Bill. But, mostly, I miss my son in the flesh every day. Knowing he is around in spirit helps immeasurably most of the time. But not in this moment, not right now.

CHAPTER FIFTEEN:

JESUS, THIS HURT

Early in the book I talked about still playing hockey at my age. The two objectives in my weekly game is to first, score a goal and secondly, not get hurt. Well, maybe that's not the right order. Last Sunday I failed miserably at both objectives. It was halfway through the game and a perfect pass miraculously appeared on the blade of my stick (thanks Freddie). I was on a breakaway, a rarity in itself. I was moving in on the goalie and looked down to insure the proper placement of the puck over his right shoulder. Yeah, for all you hockey players groaning right now, aware that the looking down part violated everything all your coaches taught you. "Keep your head up!!!"

Well, I didn't. The goalie decided his best option was to advance and skated out to poke check the puck just as I was concentrating on that same rubber disk. The next thing I knew I was horizontal and flying through the air as quickly as 190 pounds can travel. I hit the ice with a thud, a lot of the impact settling on my already injured right elbow. (now that the season's over I can get the bursa sac drained.) The landing was abrupt and horrifically painful. And I really didn't know if I would be okay.

That's the best way I can describe when the grief hits me. It consumes my whole being. My NOW is all pain and my future healing is in question. That's it, that's how it feels, I mean that's exactly how it feels. You're just going along and then, instantly your world is upside down. Then it subsides, leaving behind just a little more scar tissue. But you know you're alive and you are certain that you know what it feels like to love because nothing else could cause it to hurt this much.

Sally and I just got back from a funeral service for the son of a dear friend of ours. Isaac and Chris grew up together. I can see them running through the back yard holding giant water pistols; there's lots of noise, lots of smiling and lots of loving. Sitting in the temple, I did not expect to be so overwhelmed with grief. My grief, Sally's grief, Isaac's mom and dad's grief. For a few moments it was overwhelming. Maybe more than a few moments. As Cathy, his mother, was reading her eulogy from the lectern, Sally had to step in and finish. I knew what I never knew prior to Chris' passing. That longing she is feeling won't ever go away. You can only make peace with the grief and deal with the pain. We and so many other parents know that they will be your companions until you are embracing your kids on the other side. Cathy asked us to arrange for a Bag Piper for the ceremony just like we did for Chris' burial. When he was done playing Danny Boy, the piper told me that the old Celts believed that the only sound that can be heard in both worlds is the sound of the pipes. It gave me comfort and made me smile just a little.

On December 13, 2017 Chris visited. This one is very special. And I'm writing about it now on May 28 and May 29, 2018.

"Hi, Dad, lots of cardinals, that's me. Don't worry about all the things that cause you to worry. It's all fine. Follow the cardinal. Remember they don't gather into barns. Listen… open your heart. I picked the meditation music. Cardinal right. The Christmas card; it's from me Pop. You asked to be convinced it's me, Pop. How's that.

Good job on book. Did you think you were the only one we speak to? Plenty of others are touched by the other side. But you can get to others who suffer.

Feel that around your neck. That's me, that's energy, that's spirit. You're given this gift. Value it, don't doubt it. It's from me to you because I love you so much. Finally, you are back on board. You need to be on board for this to work. I'll help you. Don't worry. Look at the stream. See the shale on the bottom. Water rolls over it. It flows. Did you think the meditation music was random? I picked it for you. My gift to you. I'm with you. You're in God's hands now. He's here. You'll see.

Close Dad, right here. Rest Pop. I'll travel with you. I'll guide Marcia. She'll see me.

She will see Jerry. Way to go on really letting go. You'll get there when you get there. Once around the Retreat you and me. Thanks for loving me so much. Don't be sad Pop, all around you. You just forget.

Hi Dad, (said in his deep voice). Sound familiar. Holding your hand in the hospital in Arizona. Total connection. Love and energy. That's what it all is. But so strong and so much love. That's what I feel. Total love like you sent in Arizona. Total trust I had in you. Thanks, Pop. Made crossing easier somehow because I already knew how to trust.

I guess we connected. Glad we broke through. Keep trying, keep it up. Don't worry what they say. I'll look exactly as exactly as I did when we greet each other. Son to Father, feel it. That's pure love. Worth getting up for, right? Me giving this to you. It's not work to visit. It's my joy too.

No struggle Pop. Can you imagine? No struggle all the time, every day. This is the deal. Can't wait for you to feel it. Like Florida beaches all the time. Always warm.

I'm bringing it today, lots of it pent up. Needed the dam to burst. Feel it, Pop?

I miss you, Pop. Wish I knew then how true love feels. No fear, no holding back.

I love you, Pop. You're not pulling me away. I can't explain it, but I'm not giving up this to get that. I'm not leaving anything to be with you. It's not something you can really comprehend. But it's instantaneous when you cross. Aha moment. Lots of these when you cross.

Stay connected to Penguin. It's a pure connection. Some of my best. It won't disappear or lessen with time. We are connected by the plan. It goes on and on."

Fading back,
Love You

Well this was amazing (I'm going to count how many times I use that word in this book and get back to you.)

In every book a reader comes to *that moment* when you are either hooked or just annoyed and close the book. In the book, A *Million Little Pieces,* that moment came for me when the narrator was in the police dept holding room. It was bullshit. Remember, I'm a recovering alcoholic and I was a wild kid. I had more than a few brushes with the police. There was a charge for DWI, disorderly conduct and even Inciting a Riot. So, when I was reading A *Million Little Pieces* and James Frey was talking about his swagger and bravado handcuffed to a cop's desk, I immediately called BS. I have been there, and I was raised in a less cushy environment than this kid had been, and it scared the shite out of me. There was no show of bravado. I wanted mercy and the whole thing to just go away. Shit, I actually cried, and you can't blow your nose when you are handcuffed. Back to that moment. I hope it came and went for you early on in this book. But I pledge to you that everything in this book is true and without embellishment. It doesn't need to be embellished. I have read a lot of other books on this subject, and I know what's real and what's not.

And that's from guy who is neck deep into it and a true believer. I also want to reiterate that once I have written down the visit from Chris as it happened, I review if for handwriting clarity and look at it later that morning. I may even read it to Sally as she is getting ready for work. But then that's it. I file it in a soft green color legal folder according to the date of the visit. The next time I'm reviewing that visit's notes is the day I'm writing about it for this book. Example: the December 13. 2017 visit is being written about today on May 29, 2018 and yesterday May 28, 2018.

Why I'm describing this process will become clear. This visit is so impactful that I actually made notes after Chris has signed off. This is the first time I did that. Chris opens by mentioning cardinals. I know he send me cardinals and I've previously written about it. In fact, I had been thinking about getting a cardinal tattoo which Chris thought was a fine idea. Instead I had a feather tattoo beneath my palm tree tattoo after we wrote the song and received his poem. I was very happy I did that. I love it. But on Monday morning May 14, 2018, I was sitting in my office working on this book. I dropped my son Will at the Metra station to go to a Cubs game with his cousin, Charlie. My plan was to then head down to the city and do the responsible thing. But guess what? Well I got a psychic uppercut. Something clicked. I went home and searched for Cardinal images on the computer. I printed the one I wanted and headed down to see my buddy Dave McNair at Chicago Tattoo. Dave is a good friend and a true artist. I told him I was on my way but would only come on the condition that he actually charge me this time. He reluctantly agreed. An hour later, I was on my way home with a cardinal tattoo on my right forearm with a blue green eye and CJM on his chest. (remember earlier he mentioned initials) Getting the tattoo might have been impulsive but I loved it immediately. I just had to wait for it to heal to really appreciate it.

So, when Chris began his visit from December 13, 2017 with cardinals I had to smile. And according to my notes at the end of the page, the guided meditation by Rasa Lukosiute, referred to a cardinal in a tree. For a pre-Christmas gift, Sally gave me a snow globe with a yellow lab sitting beneath a tree with a cardinal on a branch. And I had just opened a Christmas Card (I don't open them so don't send them to me.) from Northern Illinois University that had a cardinal sitting on a snow-covered branch. That card is taped on my wall just above my autographed Jack Kemp Buffalo Bills Helmet.

I get that Sally bought me a snow globe because of the significance of the cardinal. But the rest, c'mon. And I haven't gotten to yesterday yet

When I spoke to the boys at In Balance Ranch in Arizona in November 20016, one of the Ranch kids (students) asked if we could talk after dinner in the mess hall. As we walked he explained that he lived one town over from us and, although their paths never crossed at the Ranch, he knew Chris from New Trier High School, and of course knew all about him. He told me he was coming home for a Christmas visit and was nervous about maintaining his sobriety outside of the Ranch. He asked if he could call me when he got back home and maybe we could talk and take in a meeting. We did and, as of this writing Kevin is now two years sober and working as staff at The Ranch and at Transition Living (TL). I am so friggin proud of that kid. Kevin was home for a visit for the long Memorial Day weekend and asked if we could get together. I met him at my Saturday men's AA group and then he was off with his girlfriend to a Cubs game. We didn't have time to really catch up so we agreed that I would pick him up at his dad's house at 7 a.m. on Sunday and we would get coffee, catch up and head to meeting. He even suggested an early morning cigar. I love this kid.

My plan was to get up at 5 a.m., make coffee, do some work on the book and then pick up Kevin at 7 a.m. and head to the grave for a visit with Chris before the 8 a.m. AA meeting. Timing is crucial and no dawdling will be tolerated. After the meeting I will drop Kevin off at his Dad's house, head up to the golf course to play at least 27 holes with Rick, then jump in the pool, grab a shower, pick up Bar BQ and get home in time to boil corn and make the beans for a dinner with the in-laws at 5 p.m. See, timing matters. The Normandy Invasion should have been planned as intricately.

So, check, check and check. It's now 6:30 a.m. and I'm headed to a drive though Starbucks, not far from Chris' grave. I have to return to my house with Sally's coffee pick up Kevin and then pass the same Starbucks en-route to grave. But I'm on schedule so it's all good. I'm in the drive through, cigar in hand waiting to talk to a magic board where you place your order. I'm listening to Jimmy Buffett, patiently waiting my turn in line as I hear a tapping of my passenger side window. I look and see a small cardinal pecking at my window a few times and then rest on the passenger side mirror for a few seconds before flying away. As this was happening all I could think of to say was, "Hi Buddy," and I began to smile. I think Chris was happy I was involving myself in the life of a Ranch Kid, as others had done for him. I think he was letting me know he approved, and I think that he loved me. This happened people; on the spirit of my son I swear this happened just as I described it. Just like that.

As for the rest of the visit he tells me to follow the cardinal, and that they don't gather into barns. He is referring to a reading from the Book of Matthew,

Matthew 6:26 Look at the birds of the air: they neither sow nor reap nor gather into barns, and yet your heavenly Father feeds them. Are you not of more value than they?

He also tells me that what he is telling and showing me will convince me that it's him. And boy did it. I love what he tells me, and you, about what the next world is like. What he says is very personal and very touching. I am so grateful to my son.

The day unfolded perfectly. I had a visit from a cardinal in the Starbucks drive through, I got the iced coffee securely in the fridge, I picked Kevin up at his Dad's house at 7:02 a.m. and we drove the ten minutes to Chris' grave. We sat on folding chairs on each side of the stone and smoked a cigar. We talked of the Ranch, recovery, his life, family and Chris. It was a lovely visit. We went to the meeting and I drove him home. I truly hope Kevin's parents know what a miracle he is.

Now I'm headed off for a day on the golf course with my pal and feeling very easy and free knowing Chris will be with me. It's a holiday weekend so I decided to take the highway to the course which I don't usually do, just in case the town of Waukegan was having a parade and blocking my route to the club. Heading north on Route 94, I passed a passenger van broken down on the side of the road. By the time it registered I was past it. Oh well, besides I had a t time to make. Something (I know who) compelled me take the next exit, head back south, and then turn around in the same direction I was headed. I saw the van on the right and pulled off the road behind it. I approached the van and asked everyone if they were all right. There was a driver, maybe my age, his wife and two elderly women in the back seat. I saw the tire was flat and asked if help was on the way. They said it was. I asked if there was anything I could do for them and they thanked me and said they were fine.

I went back to my Jeep knowing my son has inspired me to do the right thing and that he was pleased. To be honest this wasn't the first or last time I have done this. Most the time it involves changing a tire or fetching fuel. But I know that I have been blessed in many ways and that those acts make my son proud.

While thinking about this I began to recall a Facebook text we got from Gali, his old girlfriend (who was truly his first love), on the eve of the second anniversary of his crossing over. I stumbled through the Facebook process and found it. It makes me sad, it makes me proud and it makes me cry.

Here it is:

Jan 2, 2017 11:44pm

Hi Mr and Mrs McQuillen. I wish terribly that I could join you and Chris' friends tomorrow, but since I can't be there I thought I'd share a memory via Facebook. I told this one to William and Caroline last year but its one of my favorites. Chris and I took a day trip to Flagstaff, Arizona and when we were driving down a rural road, many miles from any town/gas stations, we saw a family pushing their car. Chris immediately had me pull over and ran over to help them. They had run out of gas and it was evident they couldn't afford it. Chris immediately read the situation and told them not to go anywhere we will be back with a tank of gas. And we did just that, Chris bought them a tank and we drove it back. Of course in the meantime while he was helping them fill the tank he was chatting it up with the father as if they had known each other for years. He never thought twice about helping anyone and being a friend to everyone.

Another favorite is when he would sing on the phone- either "You Are My Sunshine"* or "He Went to Paris" by Jimmy Buffet. He would tell me "I have a terrible voice but I'm a great singer" I think about that all the time, it always puts a smile on my face.

Lastly he used to ask me what my 3 emotions of the day were. I found it nearly impossible to do but he never let me get out of it (and he didn't let hunger count as an emotion). He always took this very seriously and it meant a lot to him that we both took the time to do this at the end of the day.

He made me a better person and I'm grateful for his love every single day. I will be thinking about you all even more than usual these next few days. For the rest of my life I will love him and identify as a Bills fan.

-Gali

* When Chris was born, he had a stuffed elephant that played "You Are My Sunshine" when you pulled the nose. It was also the song his Aunt Marcia would sing to him in her off-key singing voice when he was little.

And when I was listening to Jimmy Buffet, the song that was playing was one I hadn't in a while albeit, one of my favorites. What I didn't put together until I reread Gali's sweet post was that "He Went to Paris "was the song I was listening to in the drive -through while being visited by the Cardinal. I kid you not. I love you Gali, xoxo.

Just sit with that one for a little while.

On December 21, 2017 at 3:12 a.m. we had a visit.

"Hi, Dad, you're getting it down. I'm around you and I'm not gone. You are hurting so reach out. Count the days with Marcia. See her again, and then I'll see her. She will always be around you. She always was like an angel. She will be the same as when I was a kid. Full of life and laughter. We'll all be together. But it's not really your time. So, forget that. We are together in Naples (Fla). I loved that spot. I always felt that special when I was there. Marcia did that and so did you. No pressure, no fear, no speech impediment. Just acceptance and love. Just for being me. I loved it. I love you. The hurting is a gift. That's how much we loved each other and still do.

Thanks for that. So clear now, so clear here. Go tonight and connect to spirit. Immerse yourself in that world, my world. Find the balance of both worlds. Tell other dads it's not forever. Tell them Dad. You know what to do. You're learning to reach out. To reach me. They don't know that. Take time to write and get that done.

I haven't changed, Pop. Not really. I'll always be the same good boy ☺. This is like putting. You know how to do it. So, don't doubt it. Accept it as our path. I'm closer that you can imagine Dad. All around you, next to you. I'm not going anywhere. Give Momma my love and a hug on Christmas. Tell her to look for me. I'll be there."

Love Chris

Not much for me to say. You get it right? Chris told me to go and immerse myself in spirit that night. Jen Weigel had brought a speaker, a well-known channel to the Wilmette Theatre. After the lecture we ended the evening with a holiday sing along. Pretty Nice.

12/26/18

"Merry Christmas, Pop.

You're wasting your days Pop. You have work to do. All these contacts matter. All energy like at the grave. Their daughter is home. They know it. You got to get up when I let you know I'm here. It's our deal. I'm in the joy. Don't feel guilty about that, feel me through it. It's about joy and love. Not about your pain, Dad.

Which beach doesn't matter. The explanation doesn't matter. What matters is that I'm close to you on the beach at night. It's an energetic space. I'm there, right now. Feel it Pop. That's me. So, you don't have to miss me. Mourn me but not because I'm gone. I'm not. Marcia is close. She hears me. Tell her to listen and I will comfort her, tell her. She will immediately feel at home and the relief. She will be home. Your world isn't home to her anymore. Not really. Tell her.

Think about two beams coming together. That was us and it was real and still is real. You brought joy to the kids today without letting your sadness interfere. Good Job.

I'll be at the grave to greet my friends and yours. Lots of love. She's right, dad. Walking through the door. Dad you're my world now. Good job. Keep reaching Left over right Dad. That's our hug. Do you feel the tingle on the back of your neck when you pick up the crystal? Like a transmitter or an amplifier.

I know you love me Dad. I never doubted it. I get it now.

Caroline is starting to feel lighter and William is beginning to trust. It's a good start. I wasn't much of a friend (to them) on your side. I will try on this one. Second chance, Pop. Always a second chance. Lots of time connecting before you cross. You think you are closer than you are to crossing. Make your world better. It matters, it counts.

Good job Dad."
Go to bed...I love you
Chris

Well... pretty good stuff from the other side. Chris refers to *the daughter being home.* This has to do with a sweet family whose daughter Abigail had Down Syndrome and she crossed early. The family leaves bags of her favorite snacks (Cheetos and Fritos) in a basket over her grave for her. I was visiting Chris at Sacred Heart Cemetery when we bumped into each other. It was Abigail's birthday. They get it. Hopefully you do, too. See that's the thing. Parents who have lost kids have this bond. We drop the wall and all pretenses. We know what we are each going through and we feel a kinship.

Chris tells me not to worry about the beach. I had recently returned from vising my sister Marcia in Naples. I took a trip up to Sarasota to play golf with Allen on that Sunday. My plan was to stop at one of the beaches but I got waylaid by a business call in the afternoon. I had to head back to Naples, scratching my plans to hit the beach to try to connect with Chris. Then I started getting the beaches and nights of my visits the previous November confused. My boy told me to lighten up. I did get to a beach in Naples at night where I felt him with me. So, I guess he's right. We connect at night on beaches in Florida; which beach doesn't matter. But I'll let you know as this journey continues. He

spoke of our connection (his & mine) being like a laser beam. I
like that. I like that a lot. He promised me when his godmother,
my dear sister Marcia crosses, that he will be there. He didn't
break promises, not about family, especially not regarding Marcia.

Chris talked about being a better brother and friend on the other
side than he was on this side. He talked about second chances.
I'm a big fan of second chances.

Christmas was behind us. And I am grateful. Maybe it will
change but right now, it's hard to deal with all holidays. For
Christmas, Sally and I tried to take the focus off our broken
hearts and memories of Christmas' long ago and keep them on
our two wonderful kids. It's hard. Everything prompts a memory
and is often accompanied by a quickly wiped tear or worse…

But we came through it and the kids had a nice Christmas.
We limited our participation in festivities, but we did attend a
lovely Christmas brunch at my in-laws. They are so loving and
so sensitive. It makes it easier that they get it.

The next event on the calendar is my birthday. I don't really care about birthdays to begin with. But the fact that my son was buried the day before my birthday sealed it for me forever. Please no birthday celebration. I am absolutely fine though with using my birthday as an excuse for a late January or early February boys golf trip to Florida.

If you ask any parent who has a child, he or she would say that all holidays are less cause for celebration and more an exercise to get through them, somehow. Christmas, Easter, even 4th of July brings back memories of sparklers, small town parades and fireworks together. Easter egg hunts, Thanks giving dinners and touch football. Halloween is a gut punch as seeing children run through the neighborhood in creative colorful costumes brings back years of memories and of your child running around as a Power Ranger or my personal favorite, bulldozer driver, which was Chris' name for his construction worker costume complete with hard hat. The list goes on and on. If you have lost a child, I'm so sorry and I know just how you feel.

On December 31, 2017 I took time away from my New Year's Eve Celebration to visit with Chris.

I'm just kidding. I think I was in bed by 11 p.m. so I had four full ours before we talked. I never liked New Year's Eve. My old man used to call it amateur night. For us full time party boys, it was an inconvenience. Bars were packed and prices were increased. And, the pressure to have a good time was daunting. I never did. I can look back and pick out a handful of great Christmases; I can give you names and dates of great spring breaks. But I don't believe I ever really had a fun New Year's Eve. Then when I became a parent I realized the sheer terror this holiday must have brought to my parents. And now I was experiencing it. Drunken fights, car wrecks etc. It was a huge relief when the kids were accounted for by Jan 1.

Ames, Iowa

"Hi, Pop."

"Getting Close. Don't get too hung up on the date. It's just a number or a date. No time here. Not really. Not like you know it. It's just being. It's just always tough to get. I know. It's all revealed when you come home. (I've) Been reaching out to you. Not because I need to talk but because you do. Holiday's, anniversary, stress etc. I get it. I sent you the Buddha's message to just let go. You are only getting it now. Better late than never. And I thought I was the slow learner! Just kidding. Love you!

    You've been hibernating to stop the pain. Get going next two days. Get the book finished. Sad time I know. I'm here, Dad. I'm still so sorry but I'm crazy happy. Like never before. You'll see soon enough. Don't worry about Marcia. She is getting ready and when she gets home she will wonder why she held on so long. It's amazing, so perfect. Think of the beach at night. That moment. I sent that to you to get a glimpse of it.

Crazy meditation music tonight WTF ☺. Finish it out. I see the picture. That day in Iowa. You and me that's how it will be, honest. Nothing complicated like me putting together the lacrosse net. Just easy and free like Fitz's song. You're 'A man you don't meet every day" too, Dad.

You're popular and loved over here. It will be like coming home for you. No sweat.

Glad you are hosting my friends on the day. So much love.

The room, my bedroom makes it easy to connect. My energy is all over here. Good spot. Do the cleansing here in my room. I'll be there. I will be with you all weekend to make it smooth. The love equals the pain. But it will shift. I'm around loving. I'm always going to be around you. And then I'll bring you home.

Go to bed. Get up & write my book. Get it?"

Love You
Chris

This is the second to last visit before Chris' second anniversary. It's the second to last visit that will be included in this book. And it's a good one. He recognizes my angst around his anniversary in a few days and all that went with it. I loved that he talked about Iowa because that was a very happy time for me. I often use the picture above in meditation. Our spirits were, and are, very connected and I think that photo somehow conveys that. He reassured me about Marcia and confirmed my feelings that his room has great energy for our communications. I love the fact that he was talking about putting together Will's lacrosse net. He was handy and I am not. It was an I got it moment when he took over the project. Now, he's telling me that my crossing over is in his hands. I got it. By now the nuances make sense so the visit makes sense. And hopefully for you, this whole book makes sense.

On January 3, 2018, the second anniversary of his crossing over, Chris visited. He came of course around 3 a.m., our time. But it was also about the time he crossed two years ago.

"I'm not going anywhere Dad. It's a forever thing… Relax. Trust I'm not going and never will be.

I moved to a different level. But that's like calling long distance from Tucson or California. It doesn't matter. We still connect. I won't let that connection go Dad.

It's just a day, except you get to entertain my friends and that makes me happy. Feel the chill on you neck. Still me, Dad. Go ahead Dad. Try a hug and see if it's not me. Right over left remember? Best meditation music yet. See me in the room Pop? Smiling at you. I was always happy to be with you & still am. The healing didn't change the connect. It just frees me up a bit. I see the mugs I bought you and the lighter. I see you smiling Dad. I made you happy.

It's okay Dad. Just goodbye for now. Nothing has changed. I'll calm you down now. Because I love you. I'll be at the grave and back at home. My friends will be there. Where else would I be. You know me Dad. "

"See you Later Today"
Love
Chris.

My goodness. He is something. It's been two years and one day since I hugged him in the flesh or kissed his face instead of his picture on my dashboard. But he is still with me. In a way I don't totally understand. Buy he's here.

There are a few things I need to explain about this visit. The first one is about the healing he mentioned. As a Christmas gift, Sally gave me an hour session on the phone with a psychic healer. Sally had done one a few months earlier herself and it was life changing for her.

My healing was scheduled for Jan 2, the day before his anniversary. I called into the healer at the designated time while sitting in my office. I hated it. She said Chris was stuck and she needed to help move him forward. She seemed to say that our very close connection was due to this psychic log jam. At least that's what I heard. I couldn't wait for the call to end.

And even after I was nervous that whatever she did would block our connection. I was bit of a mess. However, at 3 a.m. on the third, that fear evaporated with a voice that said "I'm not going anywhere, Dad". Those magic words let me know we were still connected.

And I believe we always will be.

During the readings going back to the very first one, he called me Dad, when things were more serious and Pop when he was being more playful. He talked about me hugging him, right arm over left. Over the last year he spoke about this. But in one visit I believe he said left over right. But I am not going to edit or change it. Either he was wrong one time with the order, or I was wrong with the hug, and that's that. I won't change or edit what was said to make it consistent. I won't mess with the results of this gift I am given. He referred to the mugs and lighter he gave me that I talked about earlier. It made me smile, and I believe it made him smile too. He knew I was nervous about the cleansing and the upcoming gathering at the grave and then our house. He calmed me down. He really did.

The day went so smoothly. Just before 2 p.m. I arrived at his grave with a folding table, a cooler full of beer, a travel humidor with cigars, two boxes of hot chocolate from Dunkin, and some Baily's Irish Cream to chase away the chill. It was 3 degrees. The place was already packed. Kids were gathered around his grave just reveling in the love. We got everything set up and more cars kept rolling in. College pals, New Trier Pals, old neighbors and friends and family.

When William showed up with Caroline and her roommates after picking them up at the train the group was complete. Sally and I were so full of love and gratitude our hearts were bursting. They were all here for Chris… and for each other. We had toasts and stories, and tears and hugs. We then packed everything up and adjourned to our home, Chris' home, to continue the celebration. Lots of food, lots of friends, lots of love. It went on until dark. Then as fast as they arrived, they all departed with promises to see each other soon, but most certainly next year. I've included a picture below. But to tell you the truth I don't need the photo. The scene at the grave is tattooed on my memory just as the Feather & Cardinal are on my arm.

Well that's my story and I'm sticking to it. As of the time I'm writing this page, it's been 29 months to the day since Chris crossed over. Caroline is currently in Peru and is visiting Machu Picchu next week. Although she still won't talk about it, she did promise me to try to connect there with her brother. I'll be shocked if Chris doesn't make himself known at that sacred place. As for William, he completed high school and will start at the University of Colorado at Boulder in September. He rejoined and co-captained the club lacrosse team, and they won the state championship yesterday. Sally is busy as a therapist, helping others, and is in the editing stages of her own book. It's about raising a challenging but loving boy, who left the world too early.

As for me, well I'm happy that there is still work to do on this book. Editing, promoting and getting it published. Chris and I will have our hands full. We will continue with our visits hopefully until I cross. And I will continue to meet with mediums, attend lectures and research the place where my boy resides.

When I started this book, I implied that I didn't care much what you thought. However, I now feel differently. Either the writing has changed my view or I'm less anxious about my story- Chris' story. But, I do care. I care very much, especially if you lost a child, or even a soul mate prematurely. Not that all losses aren't painful but the early ones really leave a mark. I was at Chris' grave today just before I sat down to write. As I opened my chair to sit down I noticed a guy in the corner of the cemetery sitting by a grave reading. We met last year and I know he also lost a son. As he was headed to his car he swung by to say hello. We didn't need to say much to each other. It was okay unsaid. We each knew. And that was enough.

I am very grateful that I was given this amazing gift to connect with my son. And I really hope it helps you navigate the heartbreak that you may have experienced. I also hope that it helps you embrace what's next for all of us. I have come out of this experience with a knowing about the other side. Prior to January 3, 2016, I believed in God and the other side. I now know. There is a big difference. I sincerely hope I have helped you get there, too.

January 3, 2018

ACKNOWLEDGEMENTS

First and foremost I want to acknowledge and thank my wonderful family. My wife Sally (who still takes my breath away) and my two kids, Caroline & William. They gave me a reason to keep going after Christopher went home. I am blessed to be loved by them. Words cannot adequately express my love for them.

My Lab Cassidy who is my constant companion at the graveside visits. (if she is intuitive enough to see Chris why can't she be intuitive enough to stay away from skunks?)

I want to thank my terrific friends who helped carry me through those dark days. Specifically Uncle Mike Holmberg, Christopher's Godfather who never left my side that very dark first week, Allen Conrad, Rick Blommer, Mike Sawyer, Jerry, and Bradley. (every day's not a holiday Brad). I want to thank Fratdog-you know who you are, and all of my friends that let me lean on them, and still do. I want to thank my family on this side and the other. I Specifically want to thank my sister Marcia. Aunt Marcia, who is Chris' Godmother. She will carry that honor with her to the other side, where Chris will be waiting for her. I want to thank Grammy & RaRa (a nickname Chris bestowed on his grandfather as a baby. Which means... well... we have no idea.)

I want to thank Chris friends, his New Trier pals and especially the kids from Northern-AKL. They have become family to us. They visit the grave, some individually and some as a group. The evidence of their visit, a memento, a flower or a full bottle of Landshark. They include our boy, their friend in their lives. Be it by honoring him at an event, or just including him in social media postings. You give us air to breath...xoxo

Thanks to the Barrasso Family & In Balance Ranch.

A big thank you to all the mediums for sharing their gifts, and channeling the ones I love, and miss.

I want to extend a very big thank you to Lisa Hagan, agent & publisher. Chris roped her in and she carried this project from that moment on, and carried this author on a few occasions.

I want to thank Lisa Hagan Books' team. Crystal and Simon (I love that cover… I loved that day in St Paul), and Sara, who is solid and kind, for leading the PR charge. Without whom (yeah I wrote that) the book sits on a shelf. Thanks to Beth… for saying yes on October 10.

And finally, Chris, my boy. I thought I was too selfish a guy to be much of a dad, but from the moment he entered my life he brought me magic and love, and I changed. His love did that to me…and still does.

Made in the USA
Columbia, SC
04 February 2019